EASY PICKINGS™
ACOUSTIC SONGS

D1493785

WISE PUBLICATIONS
part of The Music Sales Group
London / New York / Paris / Sydney / Copenhagen / Berlin / Madrid / Tokyo

Published by
WISE PUBLICATIONS
14-15 Berners Street, London W1T 3LJ, UK.

Exclusive Distributors:
MUSIC SALES LIMITED
Distribution Centre, Newmarket Road,
Bury St Edmunds, Suffolk IP33 3YB, UK.
MUSIC SALES PTY LIMITED
Music Sales Pty Limited
20 Resolution Drive, Caringbah, NSW 2229, Australia.

Order No. AM991760
ISBN 978-1-84772-270-6
This book © Copyright 2008 Wise Publications,
a division of Music Sales Limited.

Music edited by Tom Farncombe
Music arranged by David Weston
Music processed by Paul Ewers Music Design
Photos courtesy LFI
Cover illustration courtesy iStockphoto
Printed in the EU

Your Guarantee of Quality
As publishers, we strive to produce every book to the
highest commercial standards. This book has been carefully
designed to minimise awkward page turns and to make
playing from it a real pleasure. Particular care has been
given to specifying acid-free, neutral-sized paper made
from pulps which have not been elemental chlorine
bleached. This pulp is from farmed sustainable forests and
was produced with special regard for the environment.
Throughout, the printing and binding have been planned
to ensure a sturdy, attractive publication which should give
years of enjoyment. If your copy fails to meet our high
standards, please inform us and we will gladly replace it.

www.musicsales.com

WELCOME TO EASY PICKINGS™!

EASY PICKINGS is the new way to play classic songs in the finger picking style. The music in this book doesn't use standard notation. Instead, a simple system shows the guitar strings.

Chord boxes show you where to place your fingers with your fretting hand; crosses on the strings show you the pattern to pick the strings. That's all there is to it!

All the songs in this book have been specially arranged in the EASY PICKINGS format to make them as easy as possible. The first few songs have only a few chords, and simple picking patterns; later in the book the songs have more chords and a greater variety of finger picking styles. Some of the songs have been arranged in a different key from the original recording. Where this is the case, you'll need a capo, at the fret indicated at the top of the song, to play along.

The pictures below show you all you need to know!

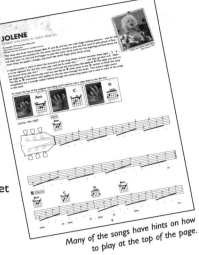

Many of the songs have hints on how to play at the top of the page.

CHORD BOXES

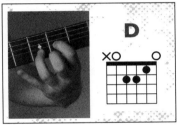

Chord box for a D chord.

Chord boxes are diagrams of the guitar neck viewed head upwards, face on. They show where to place your fingers to play each chord. Each time you see a new chord box, change to the new chord.

The top line is the nut, the others are the frets. The vertical lines are the strings, starting from E (or 6th) on the left to E (or 1st) on the right.

The black dots indicate where to place your fingers. Strings marked with an O are played open, not fretted; strings marked with an X should not be played. You won't always pick every note of every chord shape that you finger, but it is important to hold each chord in full to learn properly.

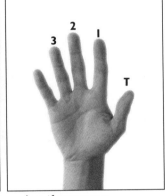

FINGER PICKING

At the start of each song, you'll see the guitar headstock and the strings of the guitar, viewed as if you were playing. The crosses on the strings show each note to be picked with your picking hand.

Usually, you'll play the first note of each group of four with your thumb (**T**), and the other notes with your 1st (**1**), 2nd (**2**) and 3rd (**3**) fingers. This is shown above some of the patterns as a guide. Follow these fingerings and you'll be playing all the finger picking patterns in this book in no time!

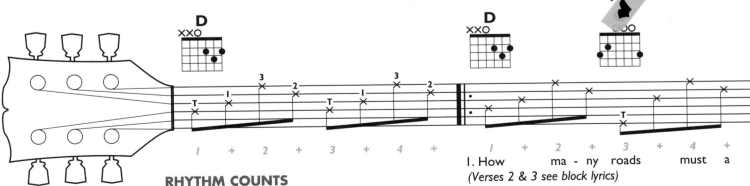

RHYTHM COUNTS

Below the strings, and above the lyrics, you'll see beat counts to keep the rhythm steady. Each number (or +) is a note to pick.

1. How ma-ny roads must a
(Verses 2 & 3 see block lyrics)

JOLENE

WORDS AND MUSIC BY DOLLY PARTON

This song uses three chord shapes: **Am**, **C**, and **G**, and has two main finger picking patterns – one for the chorus sections, and another for the verse. Use your thumb to pick the first note of each group of four, and then your 1st, 2nd and 3rd fingers to pick the other three. Look for the fingerings printed above the music when the pattern changes, and you'll see which finger picks which string.

A special system is used to show the structure of the song. Music written between these signs – ‖: :‖ – is to be repeated. For the first verse, play until the :‖, under the ⌐1._____ , and then go back to ‖:. After the second verse, play the ⌐2._____ ; here you'll see the instruction **Go back to 𝄋**. This takes you back to the beginning of the chorus; play until you see **Go to ⊕**; then jump to the ⊕ section to finish the song. The **Go to ⊕** instruction only applies on the last time through the music. This system might sound complicated, but it actually makes reading through the whole song easier, and is used in many of the songs in this book.

Jolene was a hit for country legend Dolly Parton in 1974.

To match the key of the original recording, you'll need to use a capo, fixed at the 4th fret.

CAPO: 4th FRET

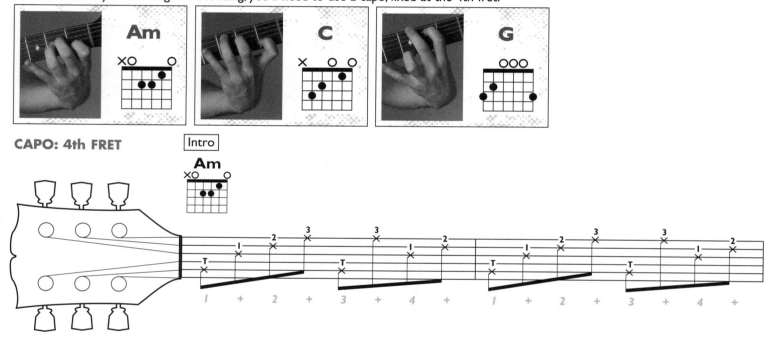

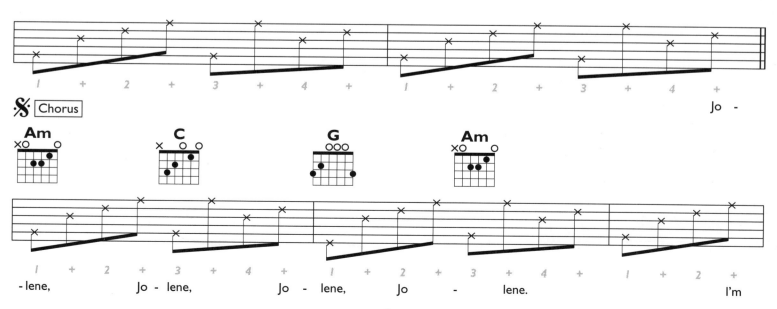

- lene,   Jo - lene,   Jo - lene,   Jo - lene.   I'm

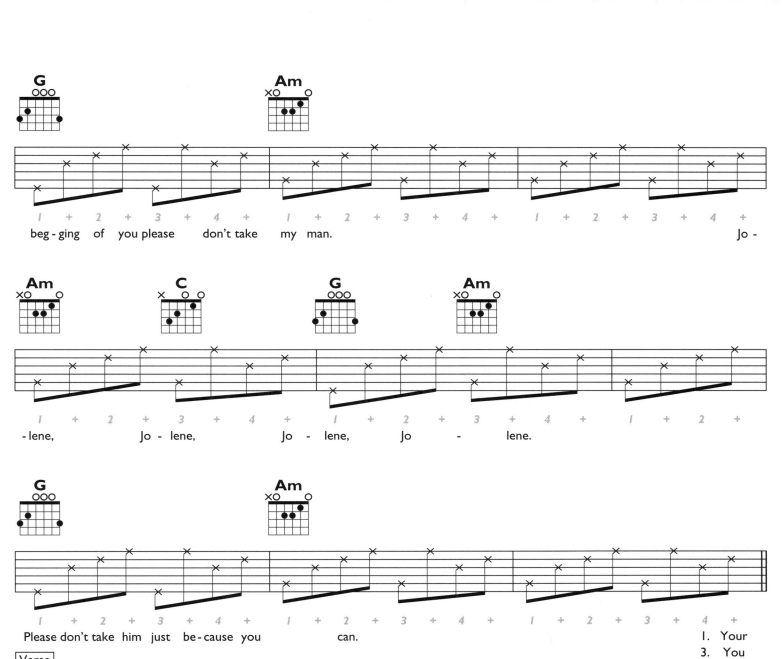

beg - ging of you please don't take my man.   Jo -

- lene,   Jo - lene,   Jo - lene,   Jo -   lene.

Please don't take him just be - cause you   can.   1. Your
                                                                   3. You

Verse

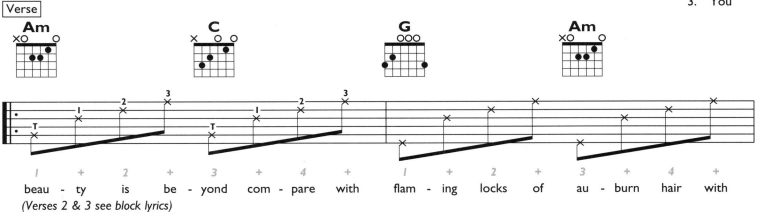

beau - ty is be - yond com - pare with flam - ing locks of au - burn hair with
(Verses 2 & 3 see block lyrics)

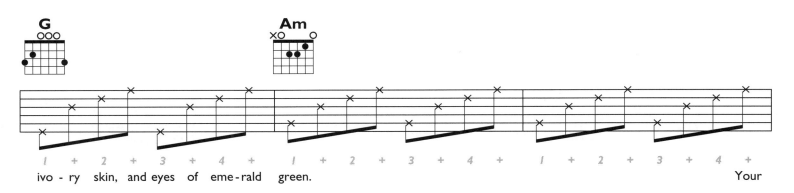

ivo - ry skin, and eyes of eme - rald green.   Your

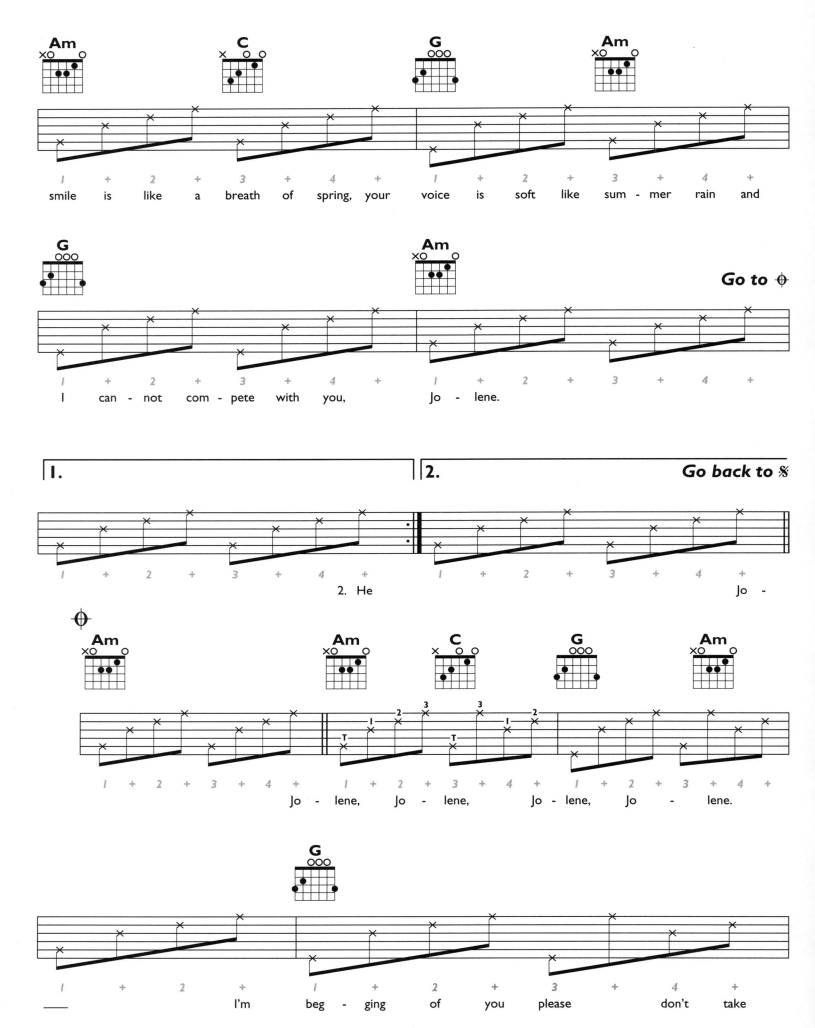

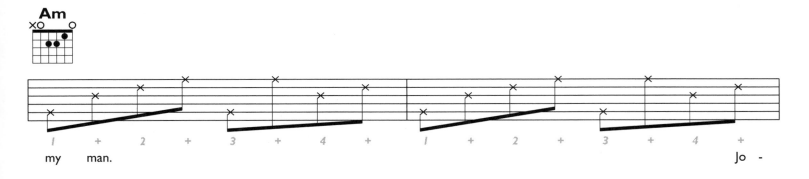

my man.   Jo -

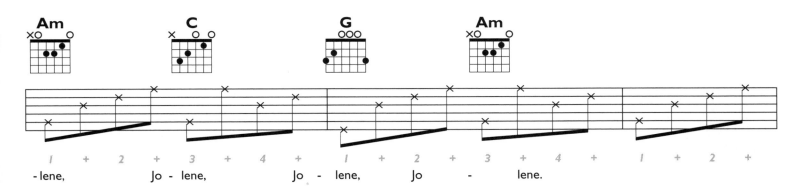

- lene,   Jo - lene,   Jo - lene,   Jo - lene.

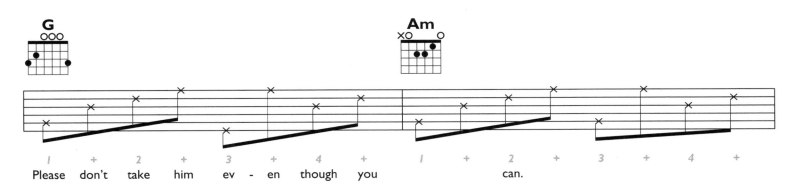

Please don't take him ev - en though you   can.

Repeat to fade

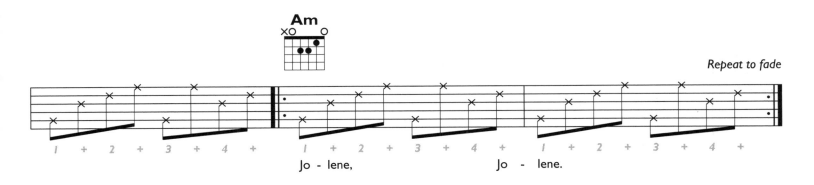

Jo - lene,   Jo - lene.

Verse 2:
He talks about you in his sleep,
An' there's nothing I can do to keep,
From crying, when he calls your name, Jolene.
And I can easily understand,
How you could easily take my man,
But you don't know what he means to me, Jolene.

Verse 3:
You could have your choice of men,
But I could never love again.
He's the only one for me, Jolene.
I had to have this talk with you:
My happiness depends on you,
And whatever you decide to do, Jolene.

LOVE IS ALL AROUND

WORDS AND MUSIC BY REG PRESLEY

The verse sections of this song use a picking pattern starting with two strings being picked together, using the thumb and 3rd finger. See the photo below, and follow the fingerings above the music to see how to play these patterns.

N.C. means No Chord: you don't play anything here!

Check the repeat signs – $\lVert$:, :$\rVert$, 𝄋, ⊕ – to work out the structure of the song. Remember that the instruction **Go to** ⊕ only applies on the last time through.

Originally a hit for the Troggs (above) in 1967, this song spent 15 weeks at No. 1 for Wet Wet Wet in 1994.

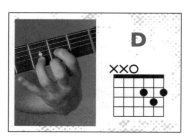

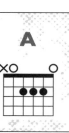
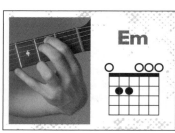

Picking two strings together.

Intro

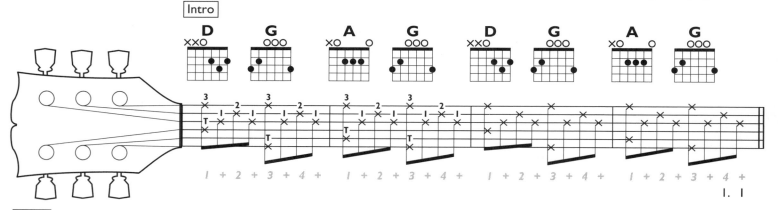

Verse

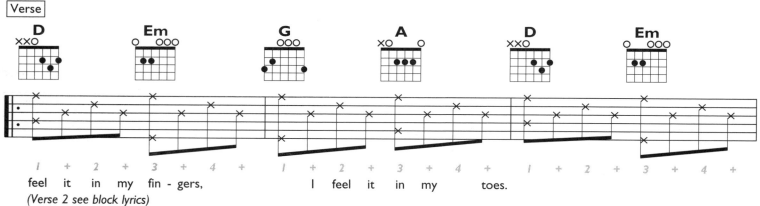

feel it in my fin-gers, I feel it in my toes.
(Verse 2 see block lyrics)

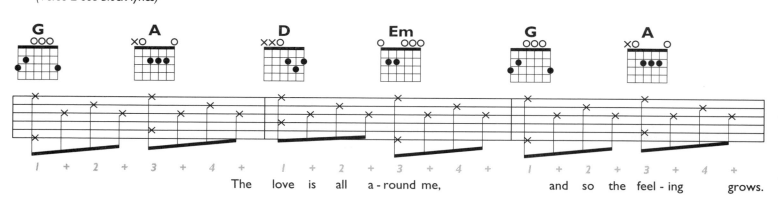

The love is all a-round me, and so the feel-ing grows.

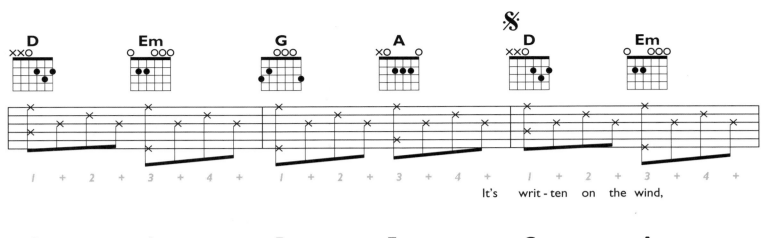

It's writ-ten on the wind,

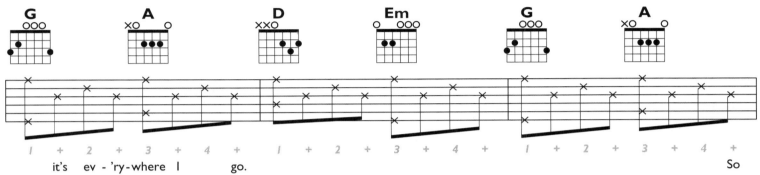

it's ev-'ry-where I go. So

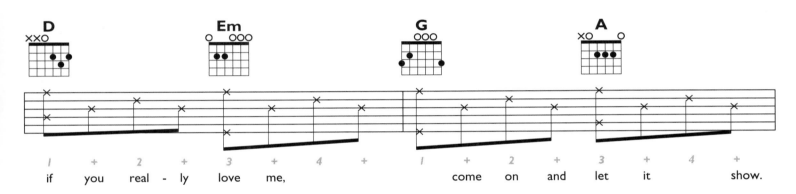

if you real-ly love me, come on and let it show.

Go to ⊕

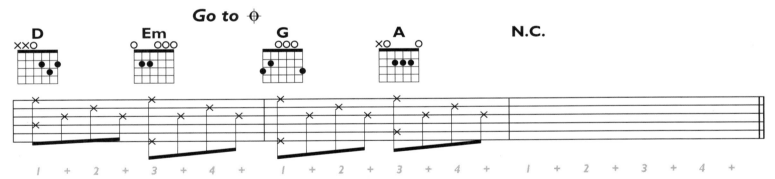

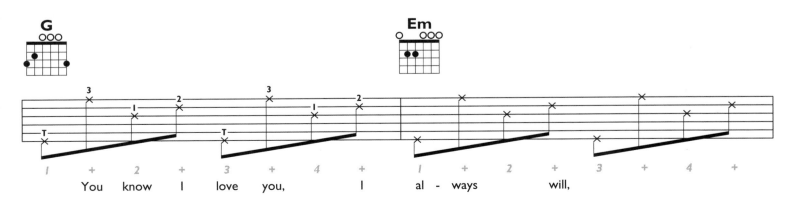

You know I love you, I al-ways will,

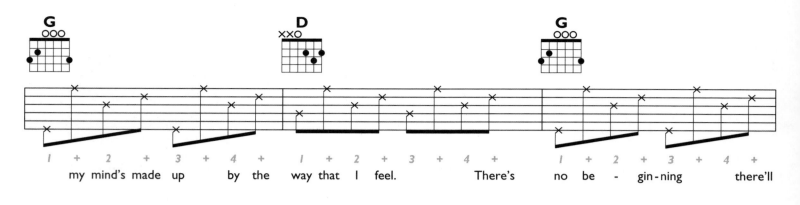

my mind's made up by the way that I feel. There's no be - gin - ning there'll

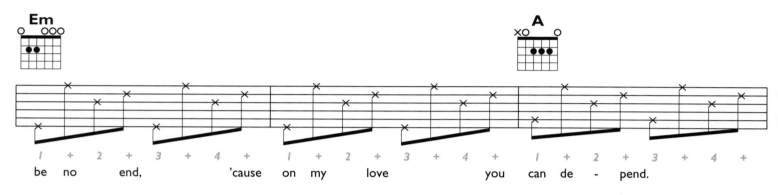

be no end, 'cause on my love you can de - pend.

1.

2.

Go back to 𝄋

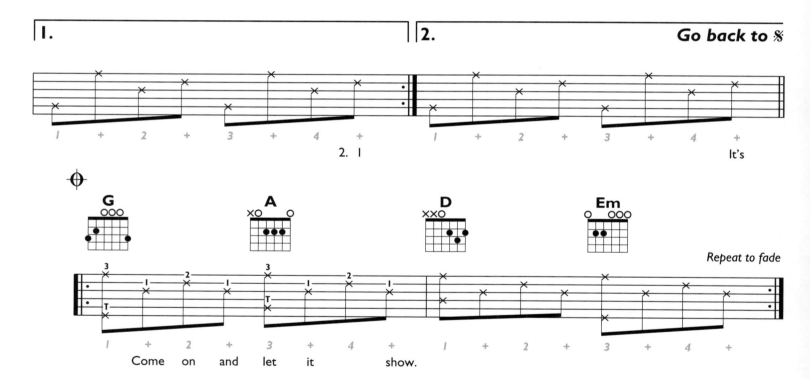

2. I

It's

Repeat to fade

Come on and let it show.

Verse 2:
I see your face before me,
As I lay on my bed.
I kinda get to thinking,
Of all the things you said.

You gave your promise to me,
And I gave mine to you.
I need someone beside me,
In everything I do.

IMAGINE
WORDS AND MUSIC BY JOHN LENNON

Follow the crosses on the strings carefully in this song. You won't always be picking the lowest fingered note in the chord at the start of each four-note group. This is to create smooth bass lines linking the chords together, such as between the chords **F**, **Am** and **Dm⁷**.

Listen to the difference between **C** and **Cmaj⁷**, and **G** and **G⁷**. Another new chord in this song is **E⁷**. '**7**' (seventh) chords have a particular sound, creating tension to lead to the next chord.

All of the notes of the last chord should be picked together and allowed to ring rather than picking each note in turn.

John Lennon's Imagine was first released in 1971, on the hit album of the same name.

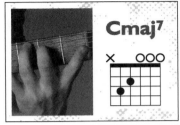

Cmaj⁷

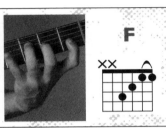

F

Dm⁷

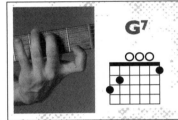

G⁷

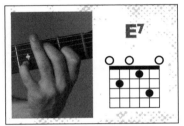

E⁷

Intro

| C | Cmaj⁷ | F | | C | Cmaj⁷ | F |

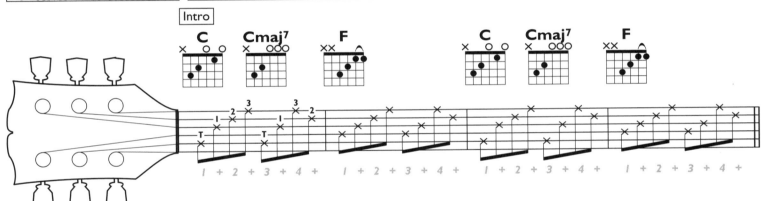

Verse

| C | Cmaj⁷ | F | | | C | Cmaj⁷ |

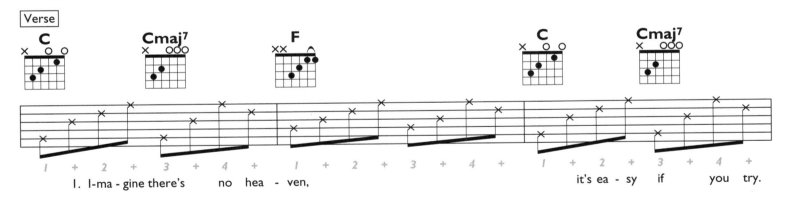

1. I-ma - gine there's   no hea - ven,   it's ea - sy   if   you   try.

| F | | | C | Cmaj⁷ | | F |

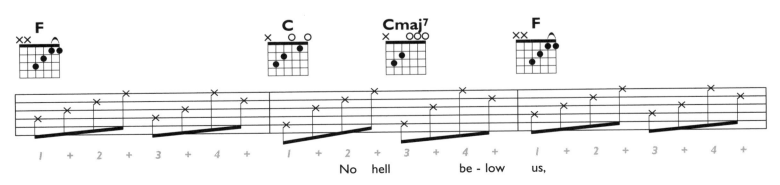

No   hell   be - low   us,

11

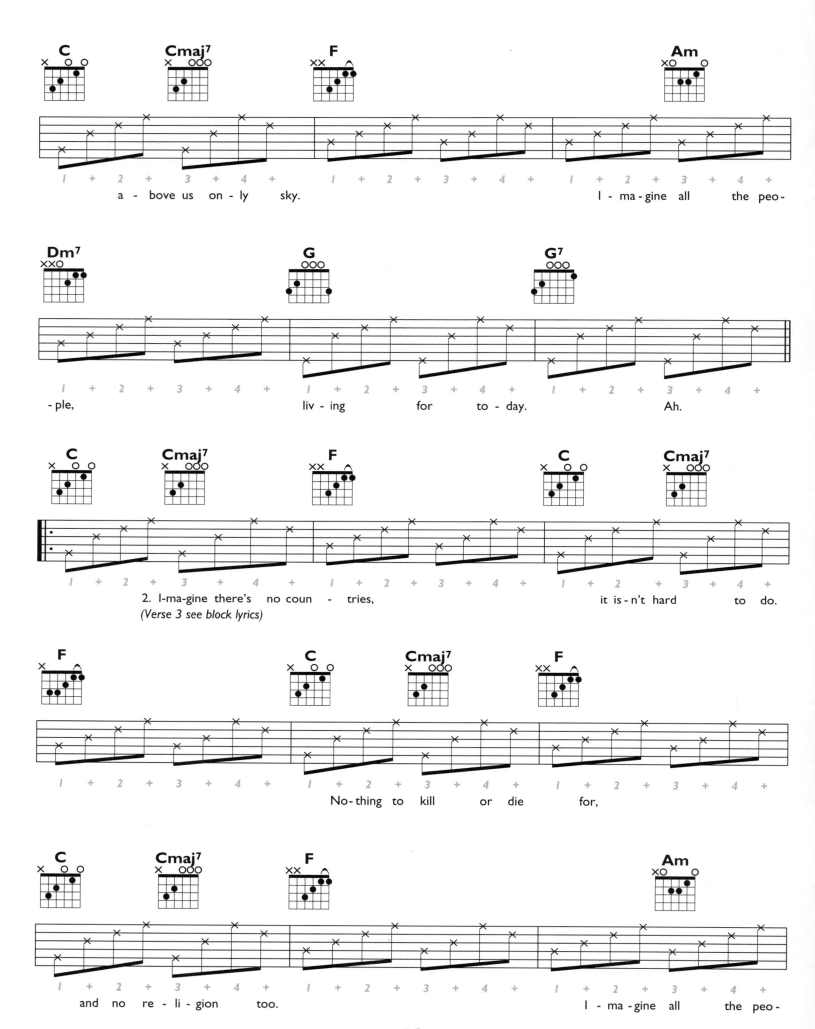

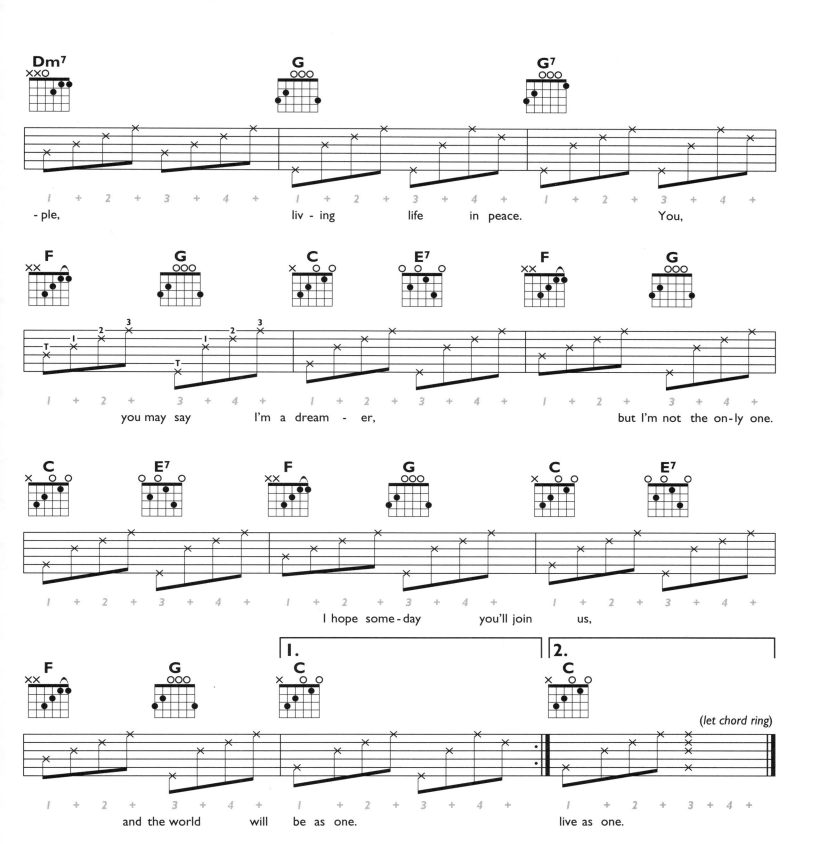

- ple, liv-ing life in peace. You,

you may say I'm a dream - er, but I'm not the on-ly one.

I hope some-day you'll join us,

1. and the world will be as one.

2. *(let chord ring)* live as one.

Verse 3:
Imagine no possessions,
I wonder if you can.
No need for greed or hunger,
A brotherhood of man.
Imagine all the people,
Sharing all the world.

SONGBIRD
WORDS AND MUSIC BY CHRISTINE McVIE

This song incorporates some two-string picking patterns, for instance between the chords **Am⁷ – G – Cadd⁹**, which are linked by a smooth bass line. Follow the crosses on the strings to see which notes to pick to make these chord progressions sound right.

Look out for the **G⁷** chord near the end of the song.

Eva Cassidy's version of Songbird was released posthumously in 1998. It originally appeared on the Fleetwood Mac album Rumours in 1977, sung by its composer, Christine McVie.

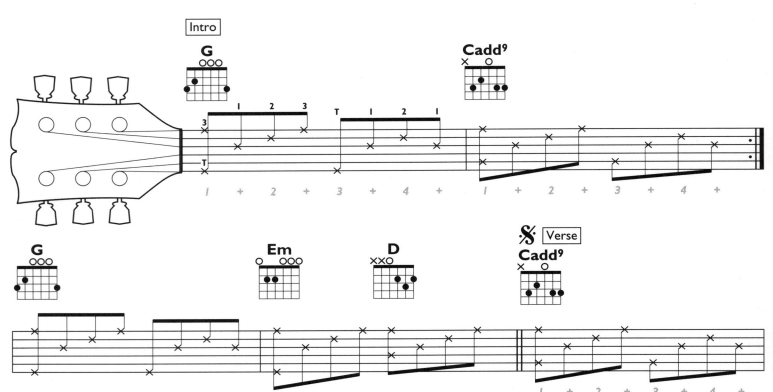

1. For you,
(Verse 2 see block lyrics)

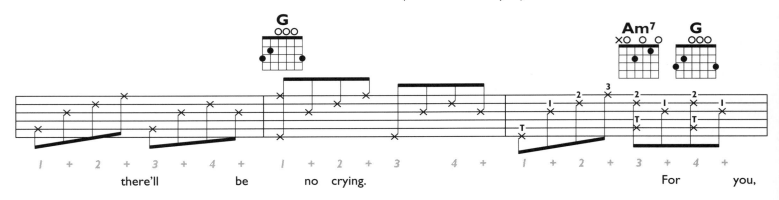

there'll be no crying. For you,

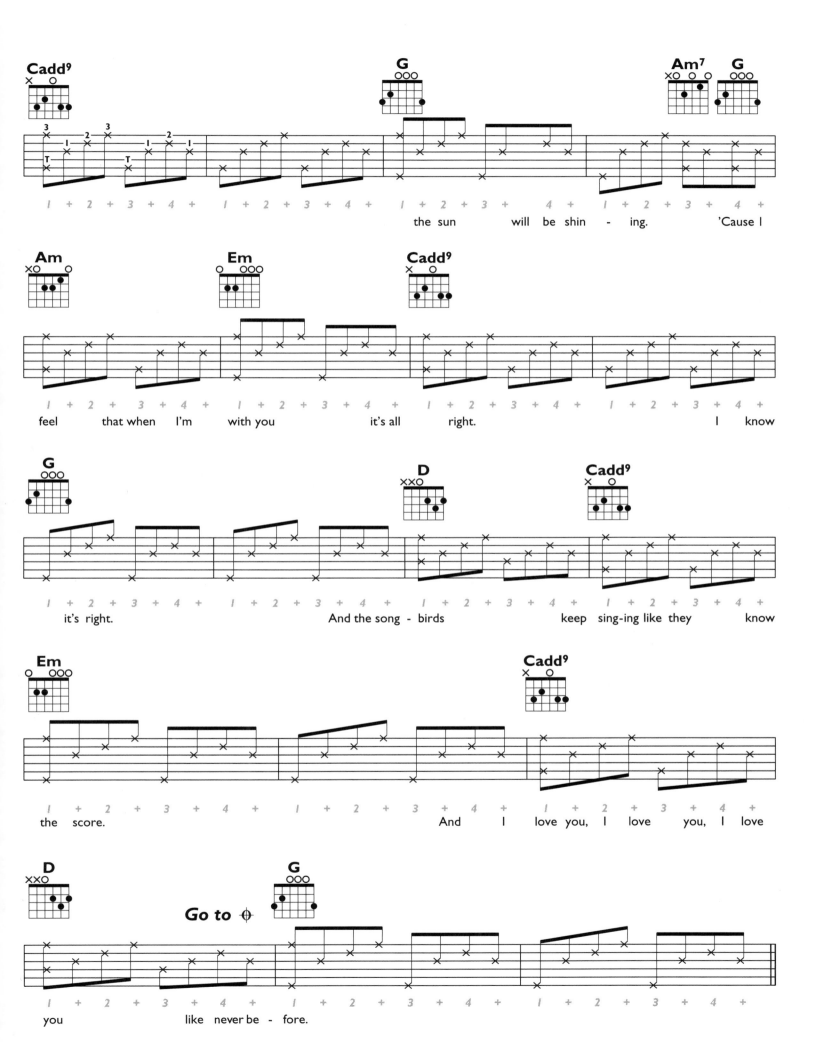

the sun will be shin - ing. 'Cause I

feel that when I'm with you it's all right. I know

it's right. And the song - birds keep sing-ing like they know

the score. And I love you, I love you, I love

Go to ⊕

you like never be - fore.

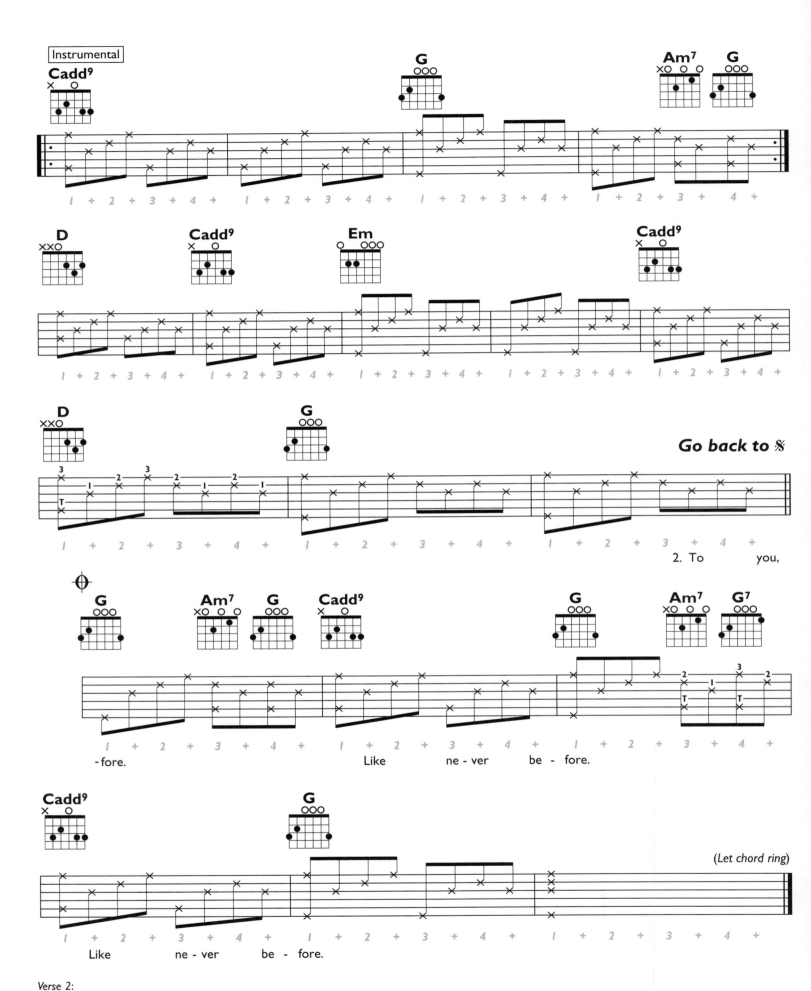

Verse 2:
To you, I would give the world.
To you, I'd never be cold,
'Cause I feel that when I'm with you,
It's all right, I know it's right.

16

FATHER AND SON
WORDS AND MUSIC BY CAT STEVENS

This song uses the barre chord **Bm**. Barre with your first finger, as shown in the photo below.

Look out for the bars which have different numbers of beats to count.

This song was first released on Cat Stevens' 1970 album Tea For The Tillerman.

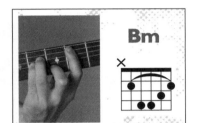

Bm

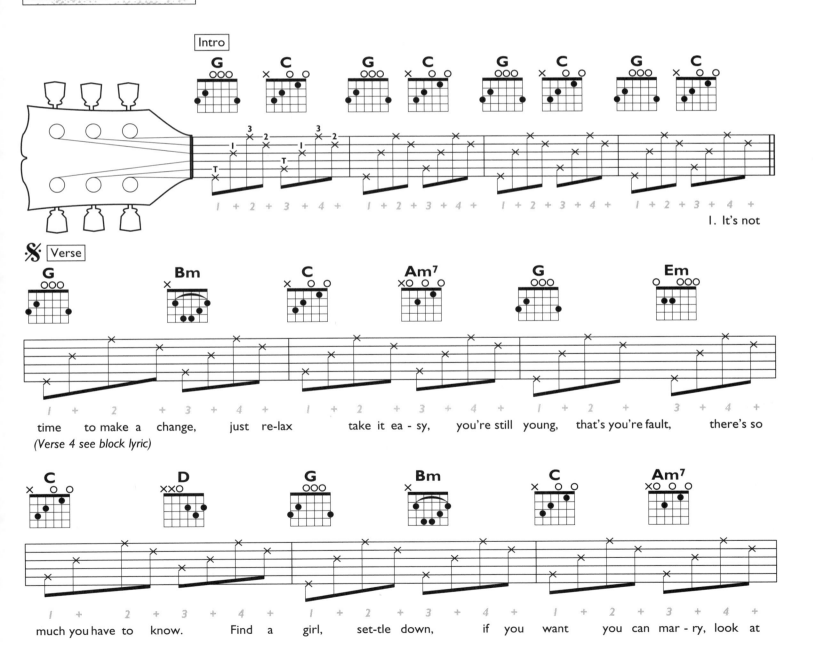

Intro

G C G C G C G C

1 + 2 + 3 + 4 +   1 + 2 + 3 + 4 +   1 + 2 + 3 + 4 +   1 + 2 + 3 + 4 +

1. It's not

§ Verse

G   Bm   C   Am⁷   G   Em

1 + 2 + 3 + 4 +   1 + 2 + 3 + 4 +   1 + 2 + 3 + 4 +

time   to make a   change,   just re-lax   take it ea-sy,   you're still young,   that's you're fault,   there's so
(Verse 4 see block lyric)

C   D   G   Bm   C   Am⁷

1 + 2 + 3 + 4 +   1 + 2 + 3 + 4 +   1 + 2 + 3 + 4 +

much you have to   know.   Find a   girl,   set-tle down,   if you want   you can mar-ry, look at

17

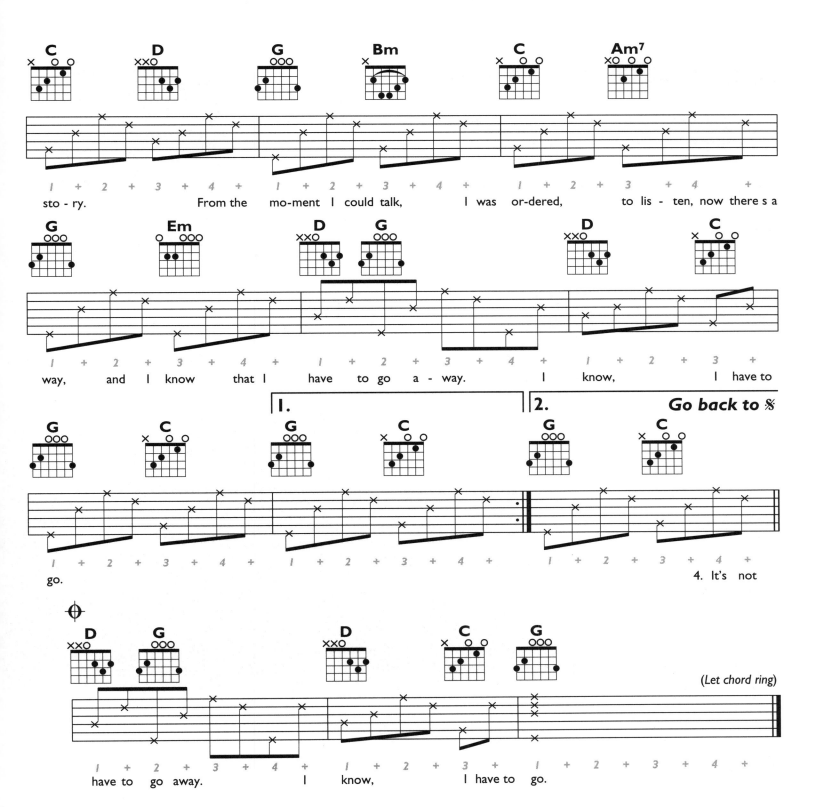

Verse 4:
It's not time to make a change,
Just sit down, take it slowly.
You're still young, that's your fault,
There's so much you have to go through.
Find a girl, settle down,
If you want you can marry.
Look at me, I am old, but I'm happy.

All the times that I cried, keeping all the things I knew inside,
It's hard, but it's harder to ignore it.
If they were right, I'd agree, but it's them they know not me.
Now there's a way and I know that I have to go away.
I know I have to go.

CALIFORNIA DREAMIN'
WORDS AND MUSIC BY JOHN PHILLIPS & MICHELLE PHILLIPS

There are a mix of picking patterns in this song, rising and falling on alternate chords. The instrumental section in the middle of the song introduces a two-string pattern.

The **F** chord in this song is a barre chord; also look out for **E⁷sus⁴**, and listen for how it resolves to **E⁷**. Look carefully at which strings to pick at the beginning of the song.

This song needs a capo (4th fret) if you want to play along with the original recording.

The Mamas & The Papas (above) had their first hit with this song in 1966. It has since been covered by the Beach Boys and José Feliciano, among others.

CAPO: 4th FRET

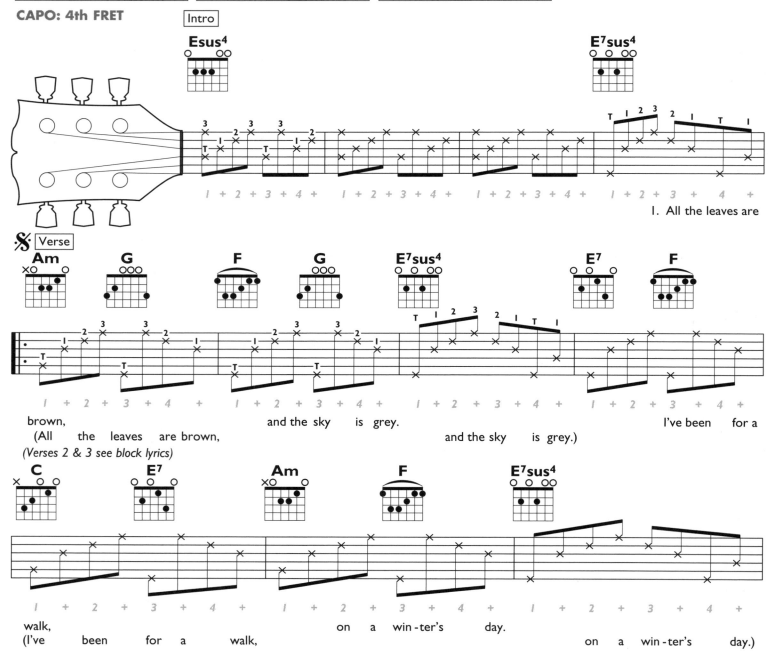

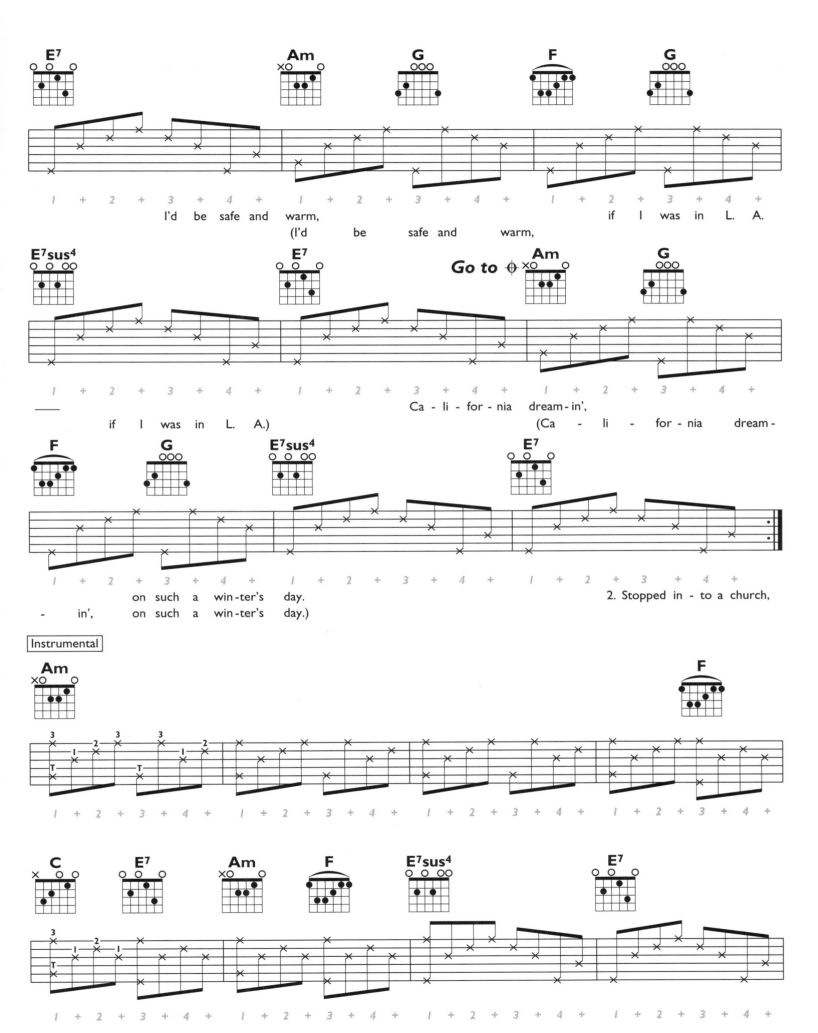

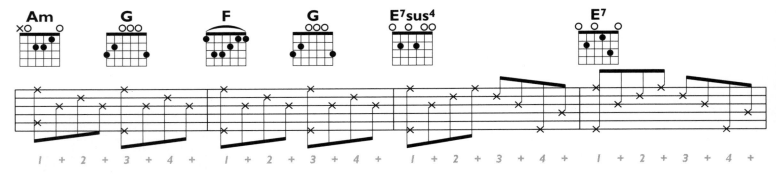

Go back to 𝄋

3. All the leaves are

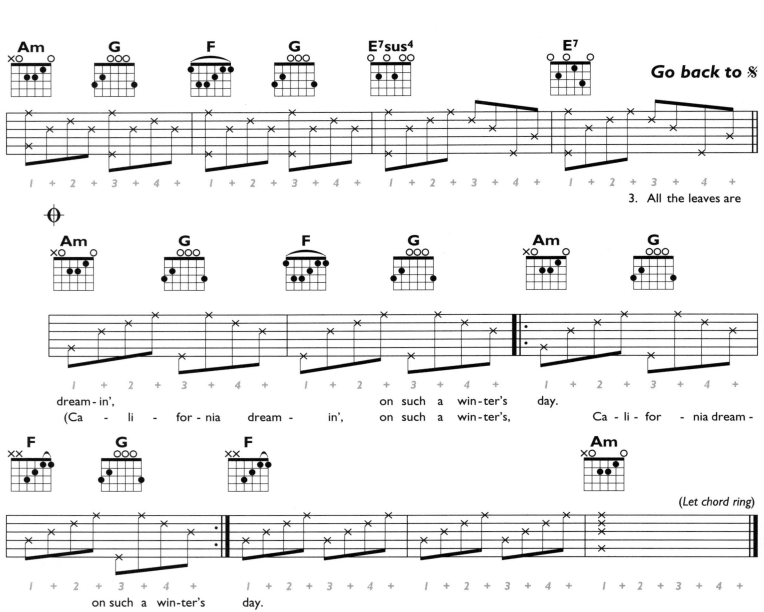

dream-in',   on such a win-ter's   day.
(Ca - li - for - nia   dream - in', on such a win-ter's,   Ca - li - for - nia dream -

(Let chord ring)

on such a win-ter's   day.
- in',   on such a win-ter's   day.)

Verse 2:
Stopped into a church,
I passed along the way.
Well, I got down on my knees,
And I pretend to pray.
You know the preacher likes the cold,
He knows I'm gonna stay.
California Dreamin'
On such a winter's day,

Verse 3:
All the leaves are brown,
And the sky is grey.
I've been for a walk,
On a winter's day.
If I didn't tell her,
I could leave today.
California Dreamin',
On such a winter's day.

GOOD PEOPLE

WORDS AND MUSIC BY JACK JOHNSON

The thumb is used in this song in the chorus to create a funky bass line connecting each chord by thumbing two notes in a row. The bridge uses mainly seventh (**7**) chords, and picking patterns which shift position between the 2nd, 3rd and 4th and 1st, 2nd and 3rd strings. Check the crosses on the strings and you'll see how this works.

Hawaiian star Jack Johnson released this laid-back hit in 1994.

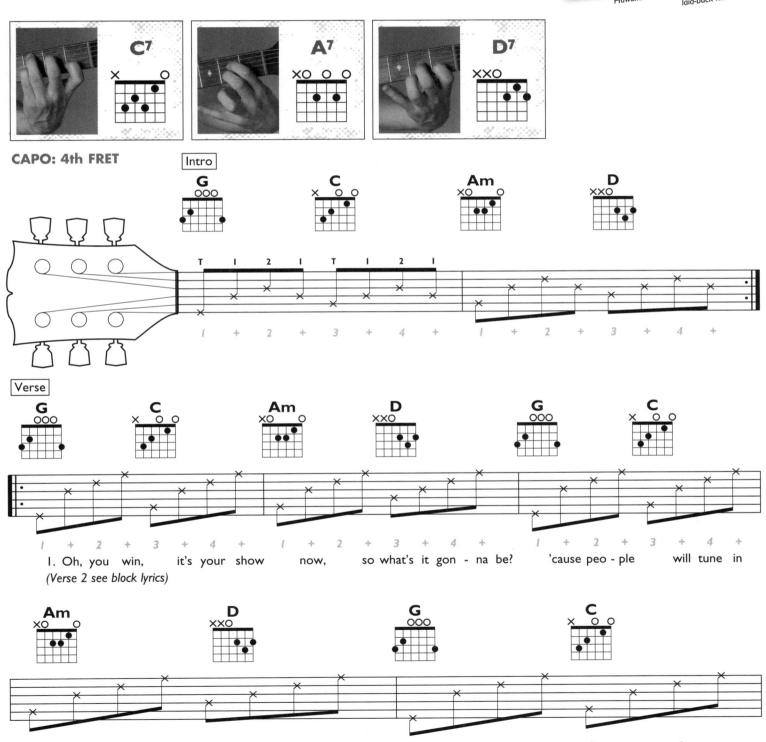

CAPO: 4th FRET

1. Oh, you win, it's your show now, so what's it gon - na be? 'cause peo - ple will tune in

(Verse 2 see block lyrics)

how ma - ny train wrecks do we need to see before we lose touch

23

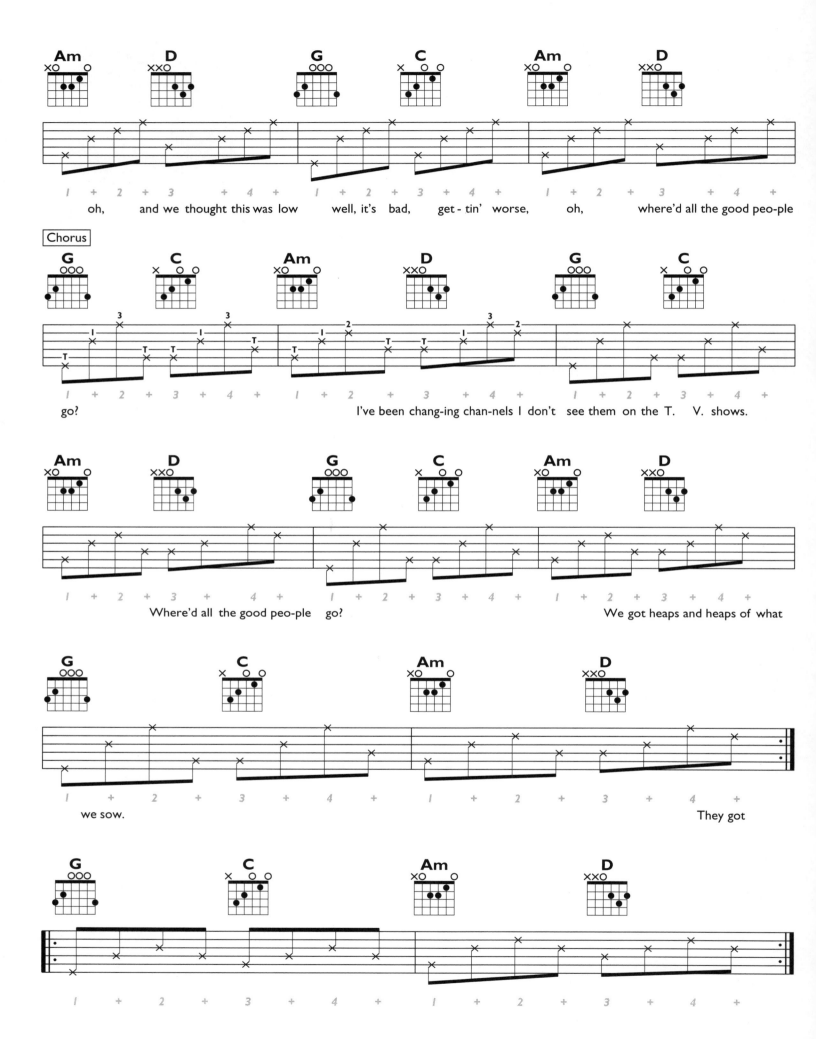

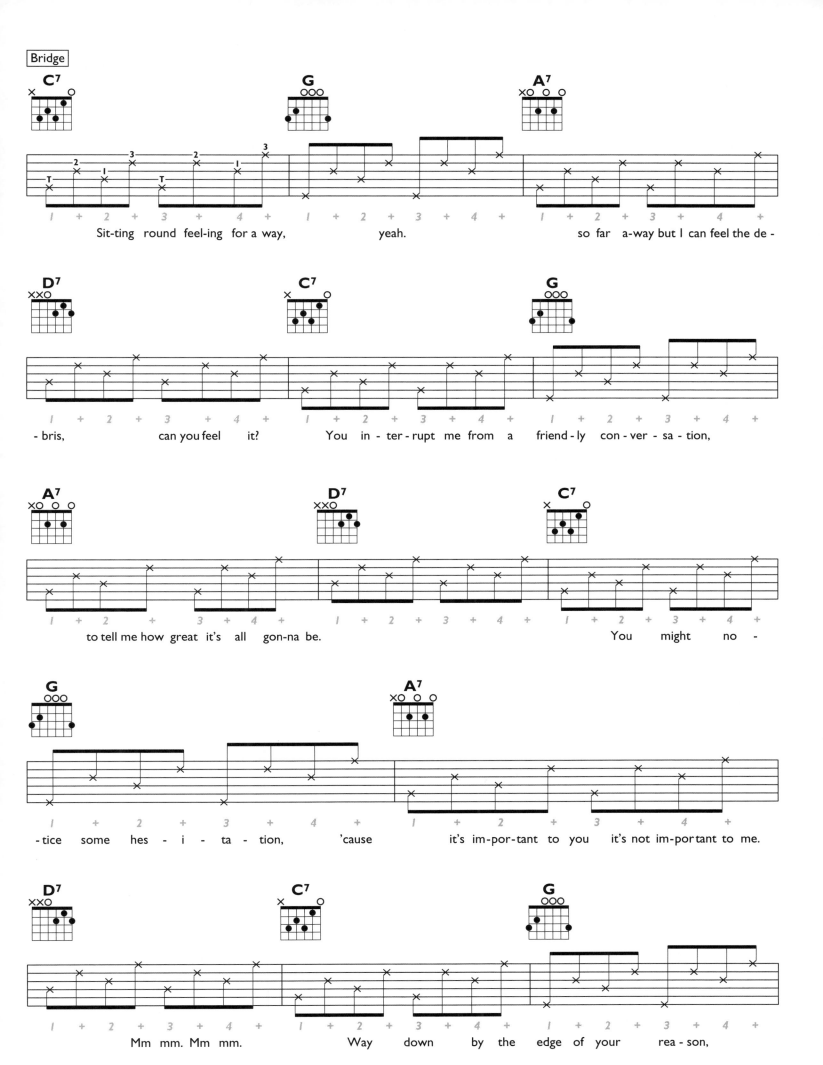

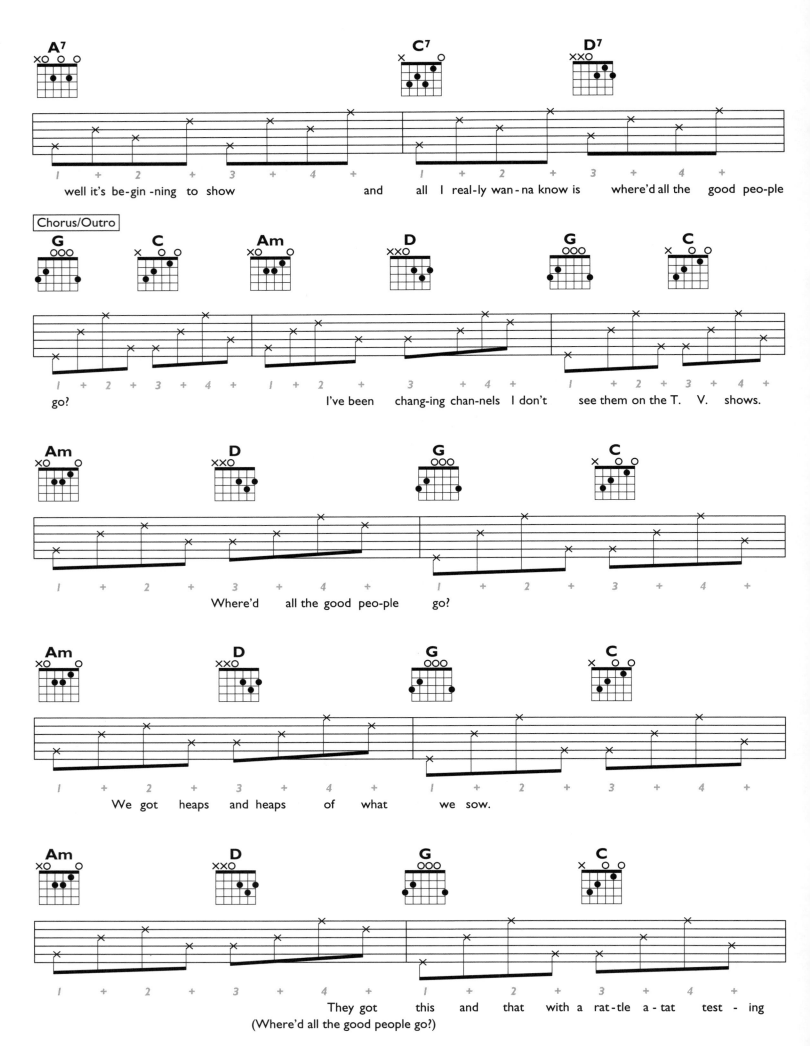

26

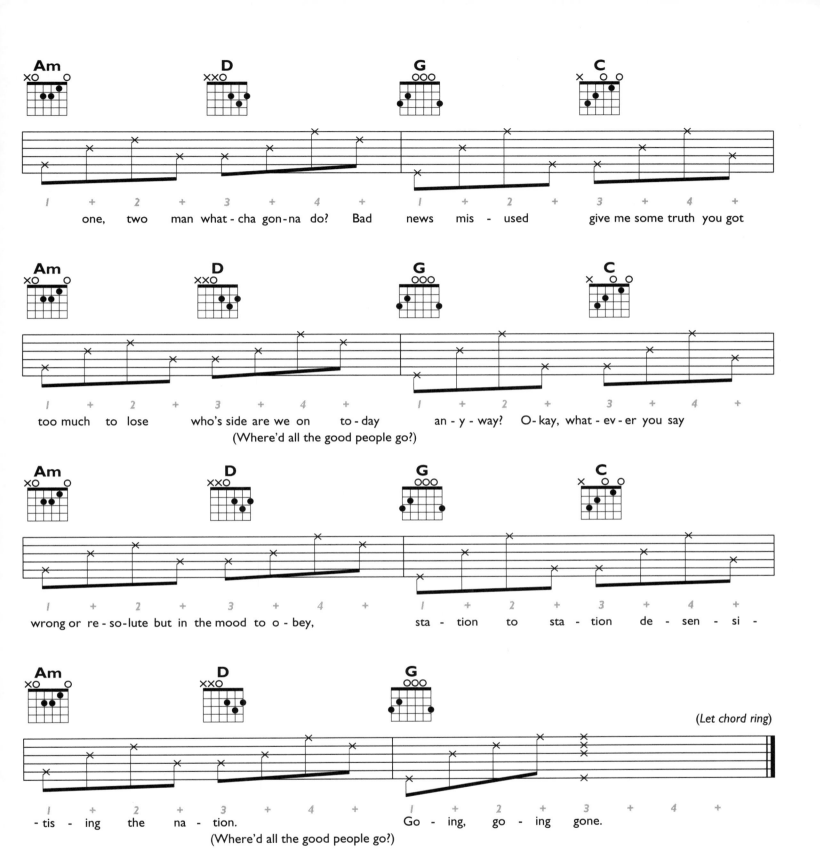

Verse 2:
They got this and that with a rattle a-tat
Testing, one, two, man whatcha gonna do?
Bad news mis-used, got too much to lose,
Give me some truth now, who's side are we on?
Whatever you say,
Turn on the boob tube, I'm in the mood to obey.
So lead me astray,
And by the way now.

A DESIGN FOR LIFE

WORDS BY NICKY WIRE
MUSIC BY JAMES DEAN BRADFIELD, NICKY WIRE & SEAN MOORE

This song has six counts in each bar. The picking patterns shift between picking the 2nd, 3rd and 4th strings (e.g. for the first chord, **C**) and the 1st, 2nd and 3rd strings (e.g. for the second chord, **Dm**).

Barre the **Dm7♭5** chord with your first finger; practice shifting between this chord and **E♭maj7**.

Welsh band Manic Street Preachers released this song in 1996.

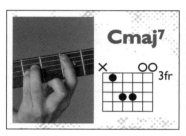  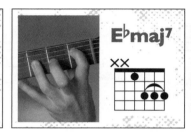 

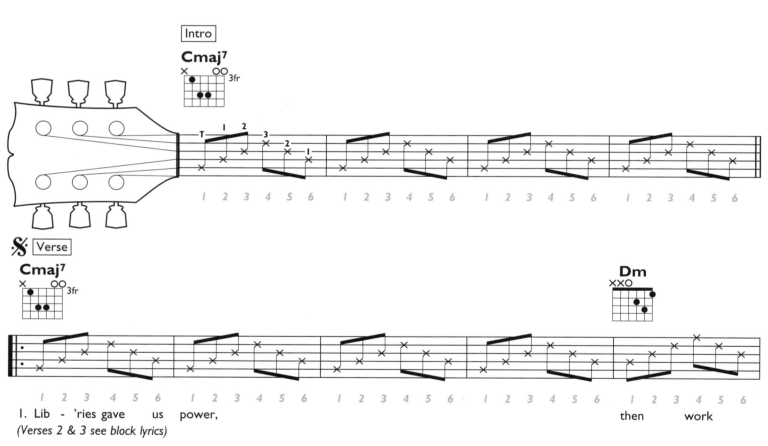

1. Lib - 'ries gave us power, then work
(Verses 2 & 3 see block lyrics)

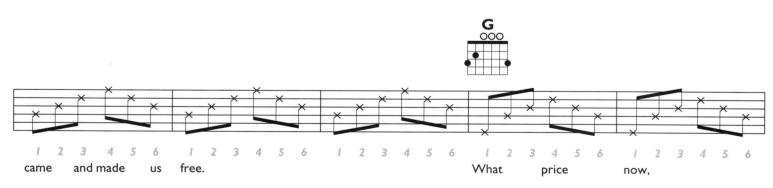

came and made us free. What price now,

28

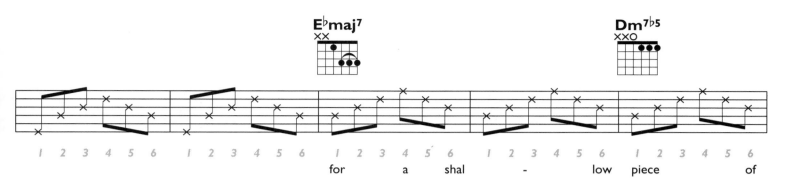

for a shal - low piece of

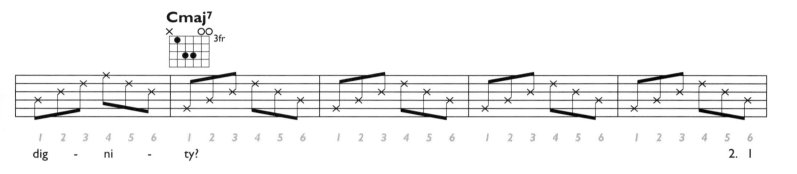

dig - ni - ty?　　　　　　　　　　2. I

Verse

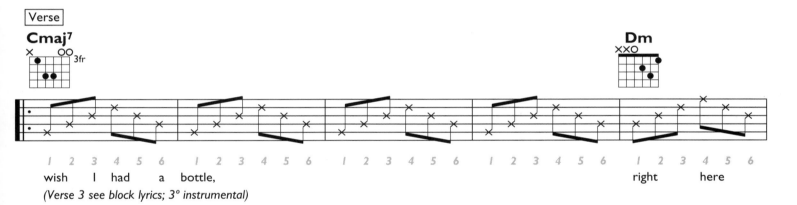

wish I had a bottle,　　　　　　right here
(Verse 3 see block lyrics; 3° instrumental)

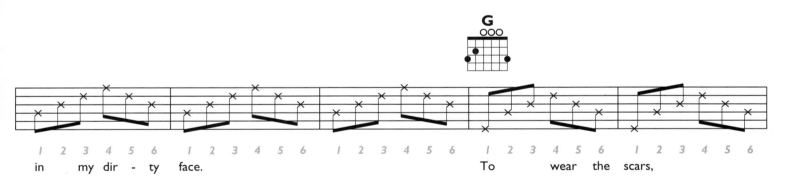

in my dir - ty face.　　　To wear the scars,

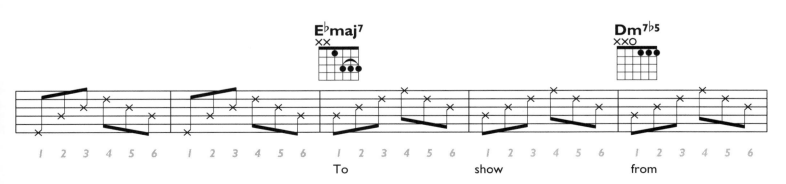

To　　show　　from

29

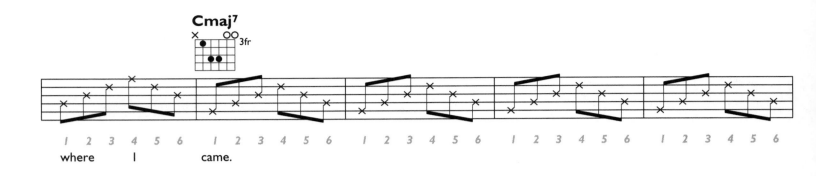

where I came.

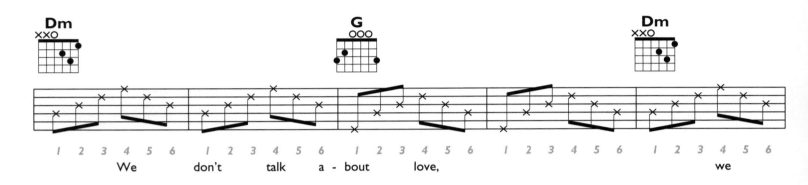

We don't talk a-bout love, we

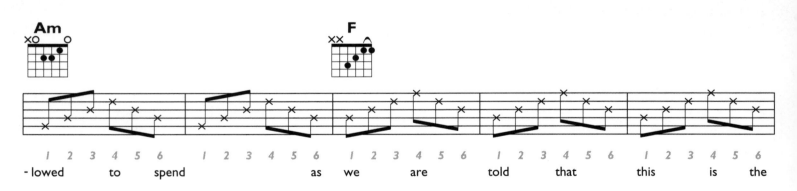

on - ly want to get drunk. And we are not al -

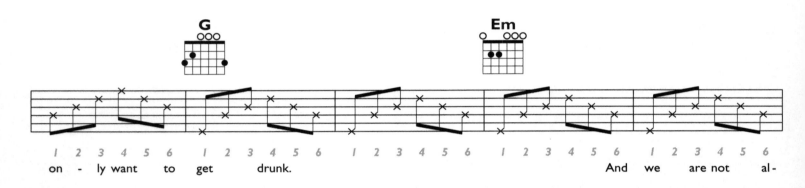

- lowed to spend as we are told that this is the

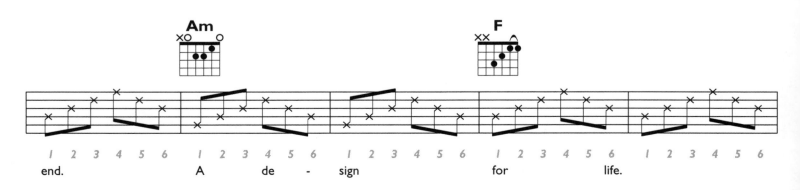

end. A de - sign for life.

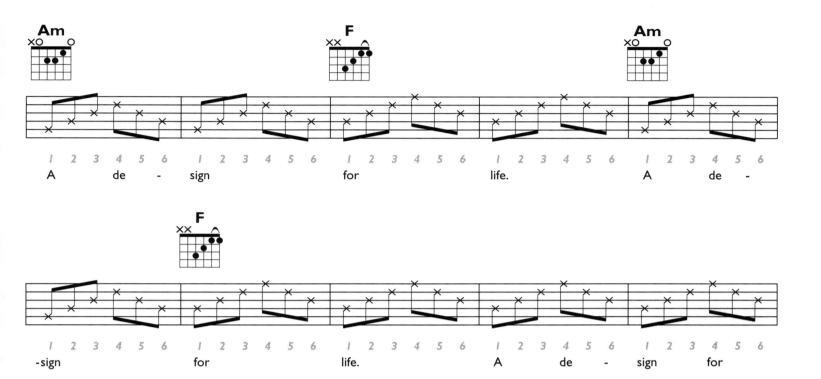

A de - sign for life. A de -

-sign for life. A de - sign for

1, 2.

Cmaj⁷

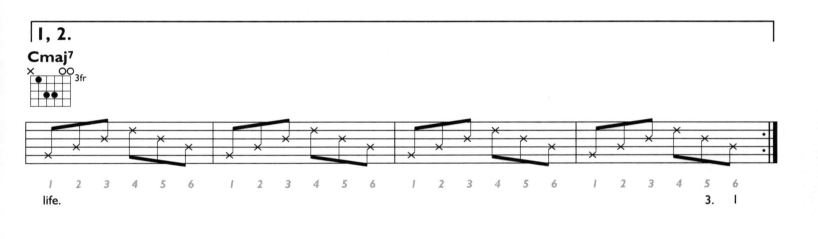

life. 3. I

3.

N.C. (solo drums to end)

1   2   3   4   5   6

Verse 3:
I wish I had a bottle,
Right here in my pretty face.
To wear the scars,
To show from where I came.

DRIFTWOOD

WORDS AND MUSIC BY FRAN HEALY

A two-string picking pattern in this song for the chorus and intro contrasts with the verses.

This song was one of a number of hit singles from Travis' 1999 album The Man Who.

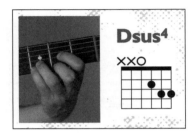

Dsus⁴

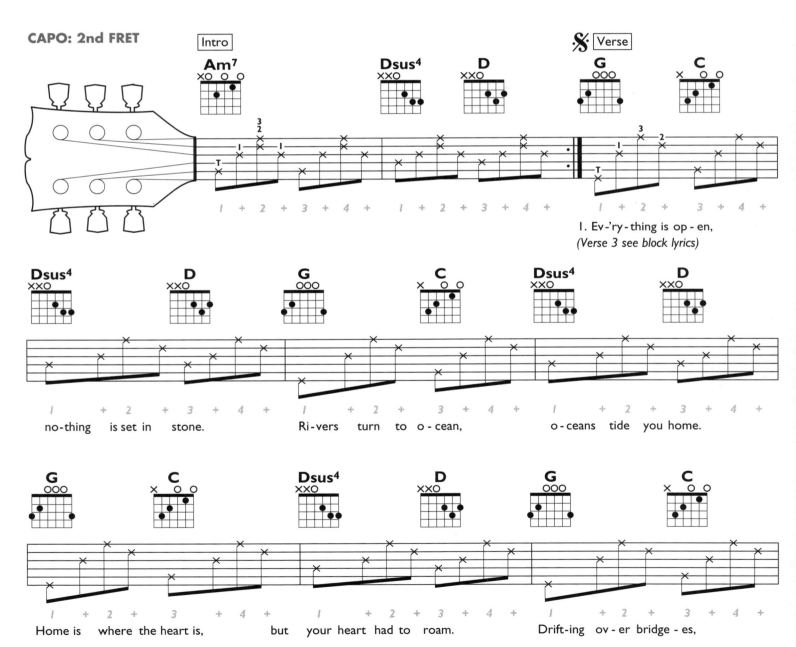

CAPO: 2nd FRET

ne - ver to re - turn. Watch - ing bridg - es burn. You're drift - wood float - ing un - der wa-

- ter, break - ing in to pie - ces, pie - ces, pie - ces. Just

drift - wood hol - low and of no use, wa - ter - falls will find you, bind you, grind you.

No - bo - dy is an is - land, ev - 'ry - one has to go. Pil - lars turn to but - ter,

but - ter, fly - ing low. Low is where your heart is, and your heart has to grow.

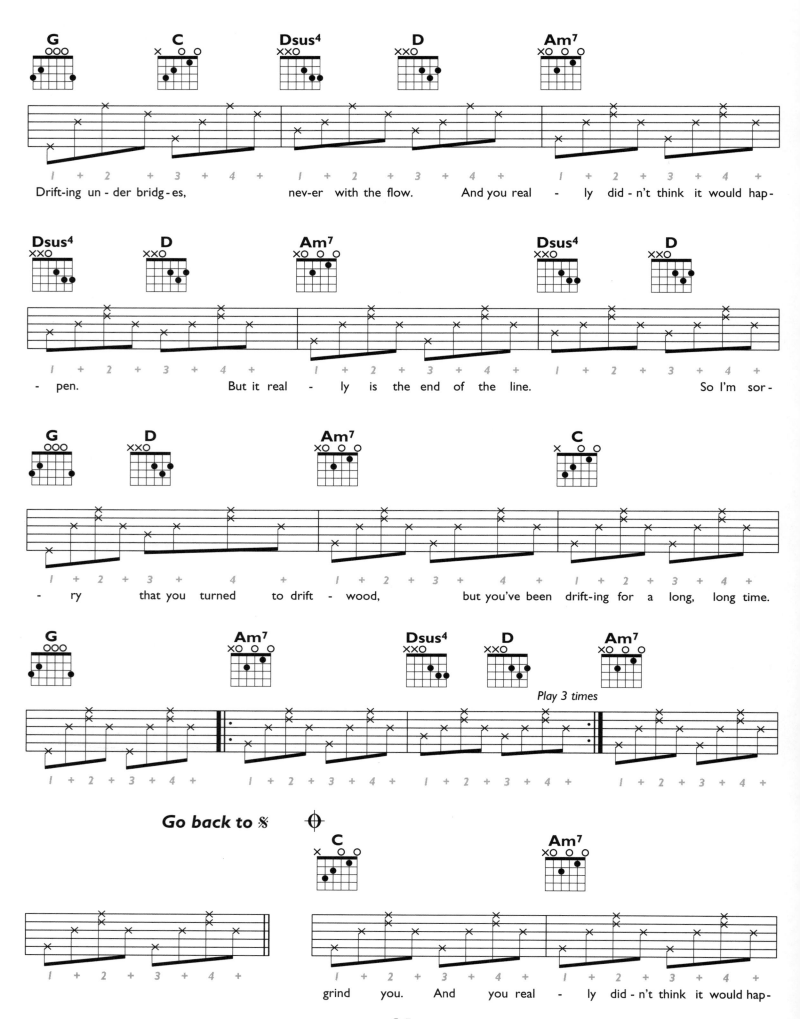

Verse 3:
Everywhere there's trouble,
Nowhere's safe to go.
Pushes turn to shovels,
Shovelling the snow.
Frozen you have chosen,
The path you wish to go.
Drifting now forever,
And forever more,
Until you reach your shore.

FIX YOU

WORDS AND MUSIC BY GUY BERRYMAN, CHRIS MARTIN, JON BUCKLAND & WILL CHAMPION

There are some quick chord changes in this song between the chords **F** – **Am** – **Gsus⁴**.

Fix You was featured on Coldplay's third album, X&Y.

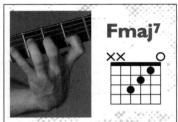

CAPO: 3rd FRET

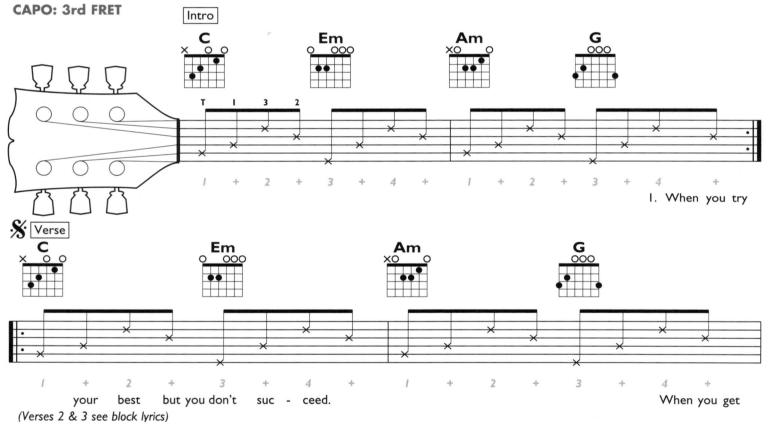

1. When you try

your best but you don't suc - ceed.   When you get

(Verses 2 & 3 see block lyrics)

whatyou want, but not what you need.   When you feel so tired but you can't sleep.

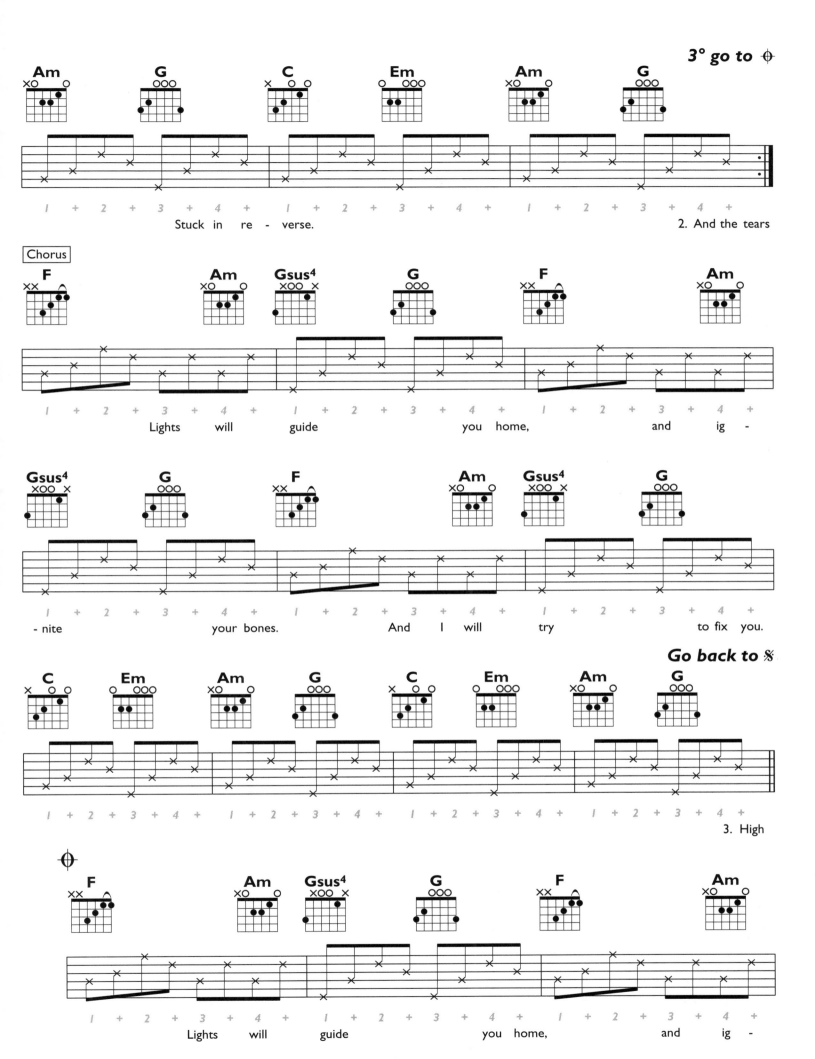

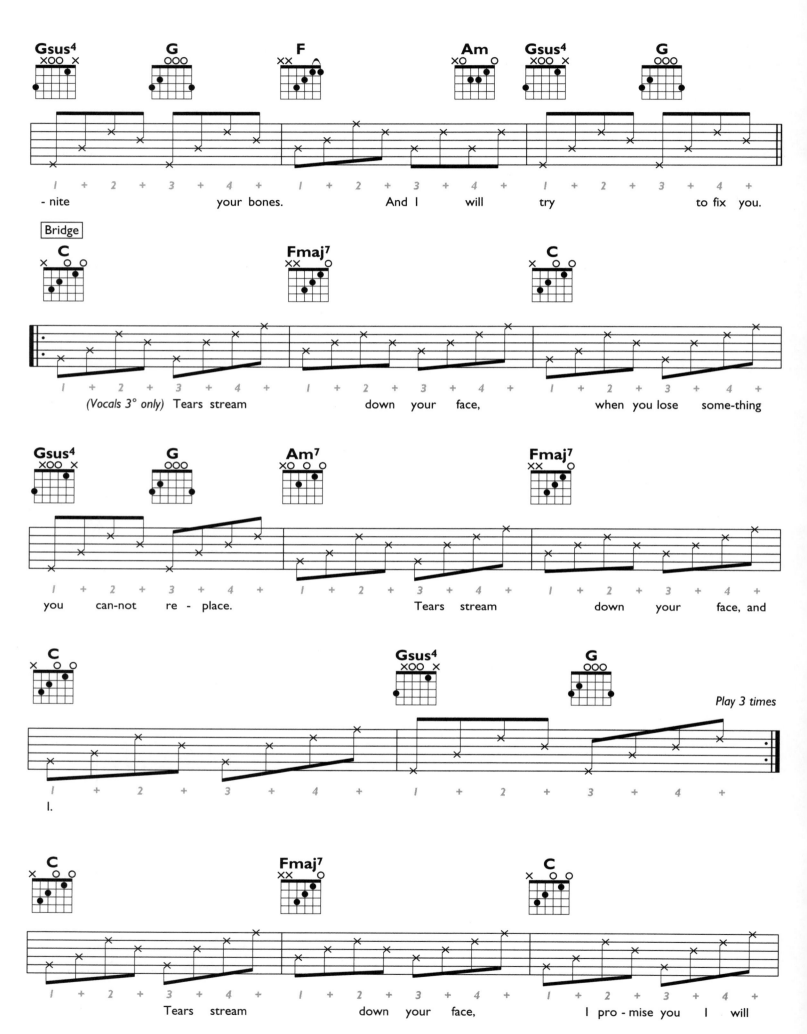

38

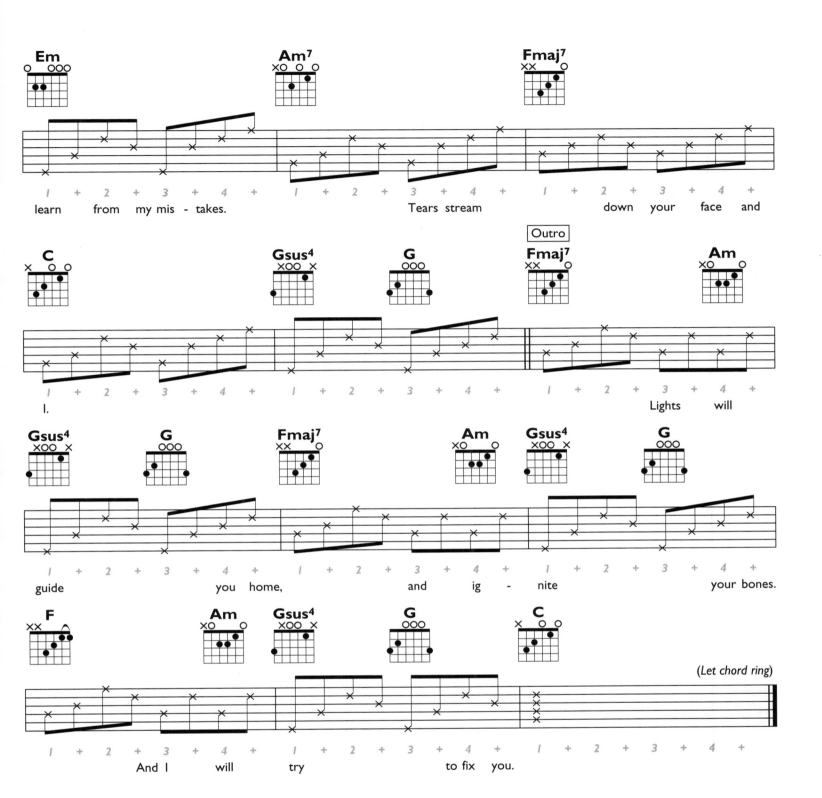

Verse 2:
When the tears come streaming down your face.
When you lose something you can't replace.
Or you love someone but it goes to waste.
Could it be worse?

Verse 3:
High up above or down below.
When you're too in love to let it go.
But if you never try, you'll never know
Just what you're worth.

HALF THE WORLD AWAY

WORDS AND MUSIC BY NOEL GALLAGHER

The picking patterns for the verse of this song have just one thumbed note per bar.

Look out for the **G/F** chord, and the change from **Fmaj⁷** to **Fm**.

This Oasis song – sung by songwriter Noel Gallagher, above – is perhaps best known as the theme song to the BBC comedy The Royle Family.

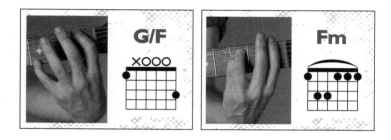

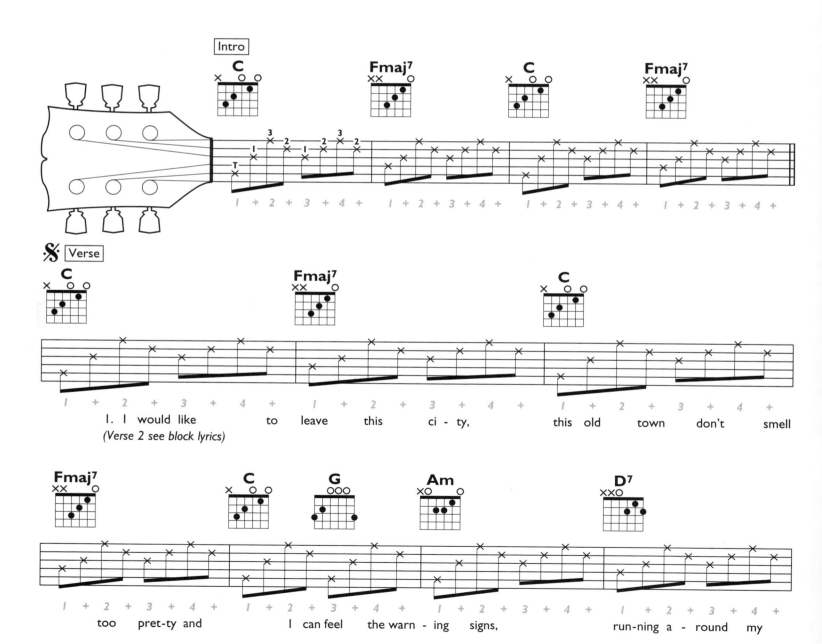

1. I would like to leave this ci - ty, this old town don't smell
(Verse 2 see block lyrics)

too pret-ty and I can feel the warn - ing signs, run-ning a - round my

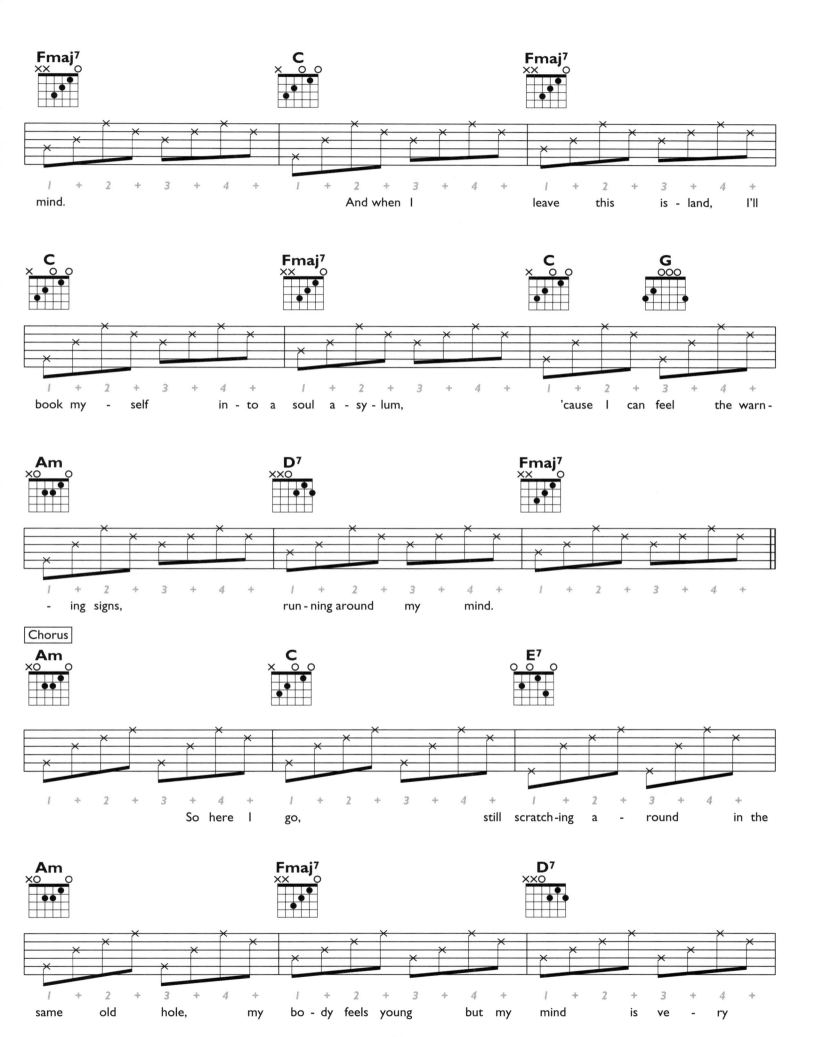

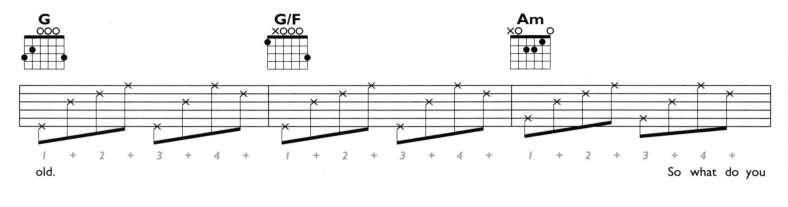

old.   So what do you

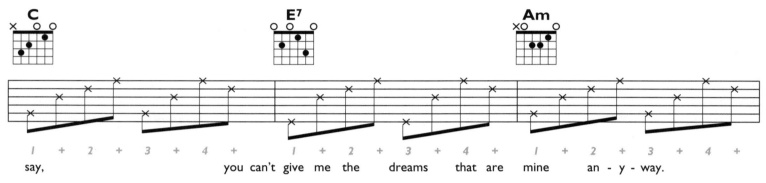

say,   you can't give me the   dreams   that are   mine   an - y - way.

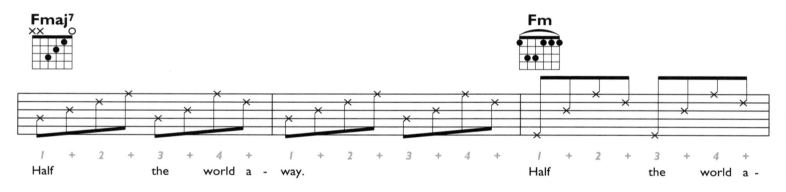

Half   the   world a - way.   Half   the   world a -

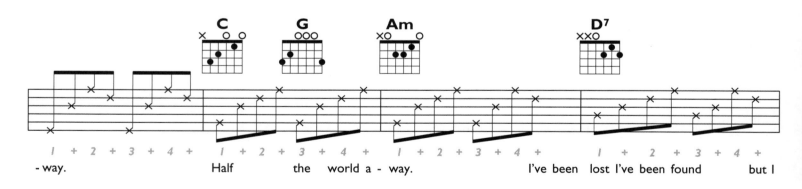

- way.   Half   the   world a - way.   I've been lost I've been found   but I

Go to ⊕

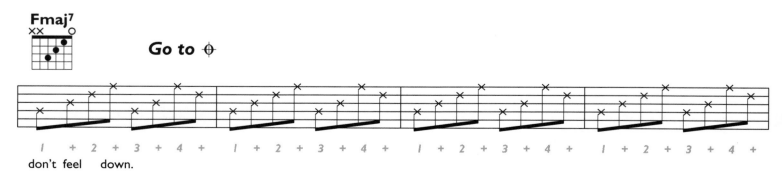

don't feel   down.

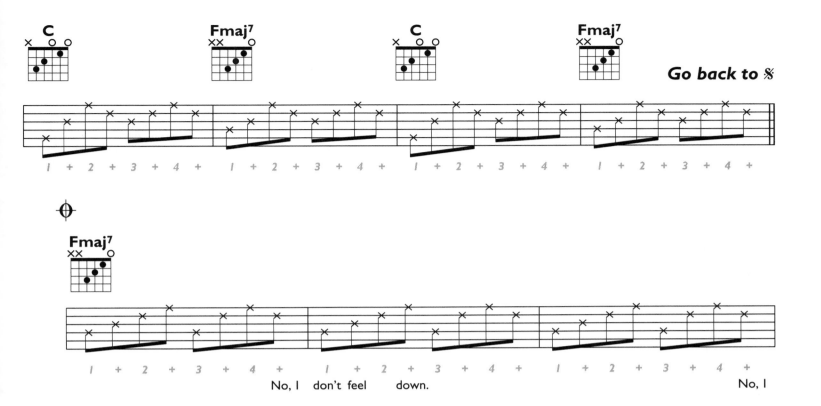

Go back to 𝄋

No, I don't feel down. No, I

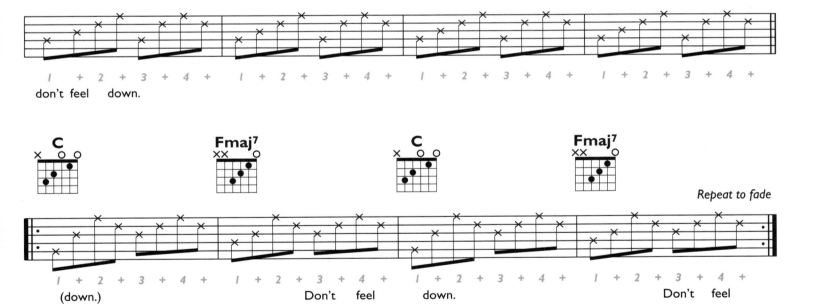

don't feel down.

Repeat to fade

(down.) Don't feel down. Don't feel

Verse 2:
And when I leave this planet,
You know I'd stay but I just can't stand it and,
I can feel the warning signs running around my mind.
And if I could leave this spirit,
I'd find me a hole and I'll live in it and,
I can feel the warning signs running around my mind.

SULTANS OF SWING

WORDS AND MUSIC BY MARK KNOPFLER

Practise this song slowly before building up to the speed of the original record! Try to keep the rhythm steady throughout the song.

The **B**♭ chord shown below is another barre chord shape.

This song was a 1978 hit for Dire Straits
(guitarist/singer Mark Knopfler pictured above).

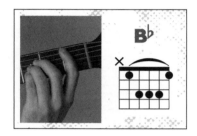

B♭

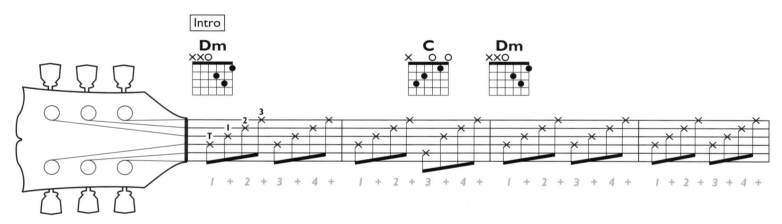

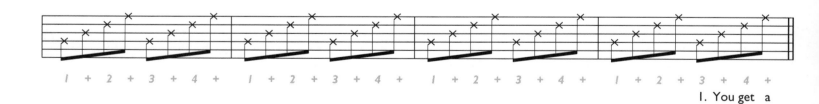

1. You get a

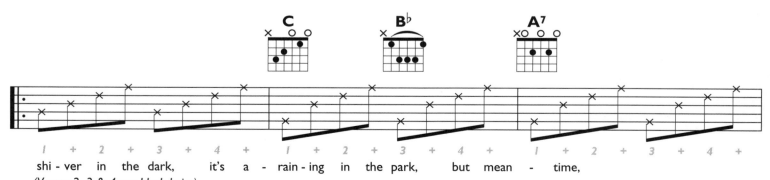

shi - ver in the dark, it's a - rain - ing in the park, but mean - time,
(Verses 2, 3 & 4 see block lyrics)

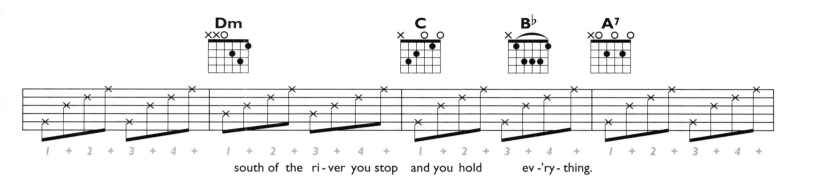

south of the ri-ver you stop and you hold ev-'ry-thing.

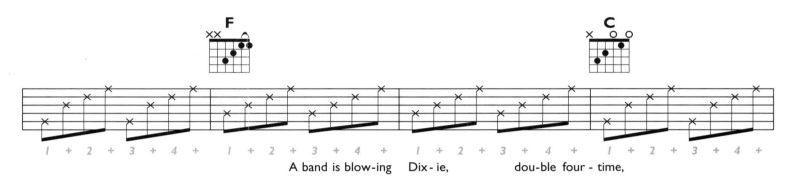

A band is blow-ing Dix-ie, dou-ble four-time,

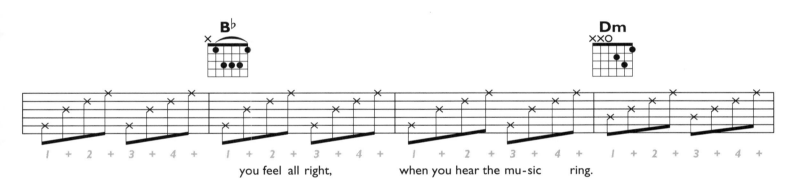

you feel all right, when you hear the mu-sic ring.

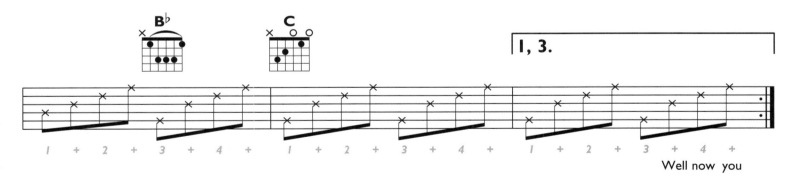

I, 3.

Well now you

2, 4.

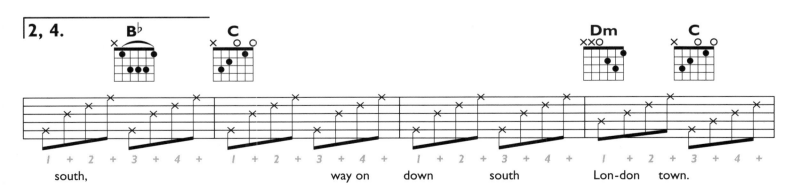

south, way on down south Lon-don town.

45

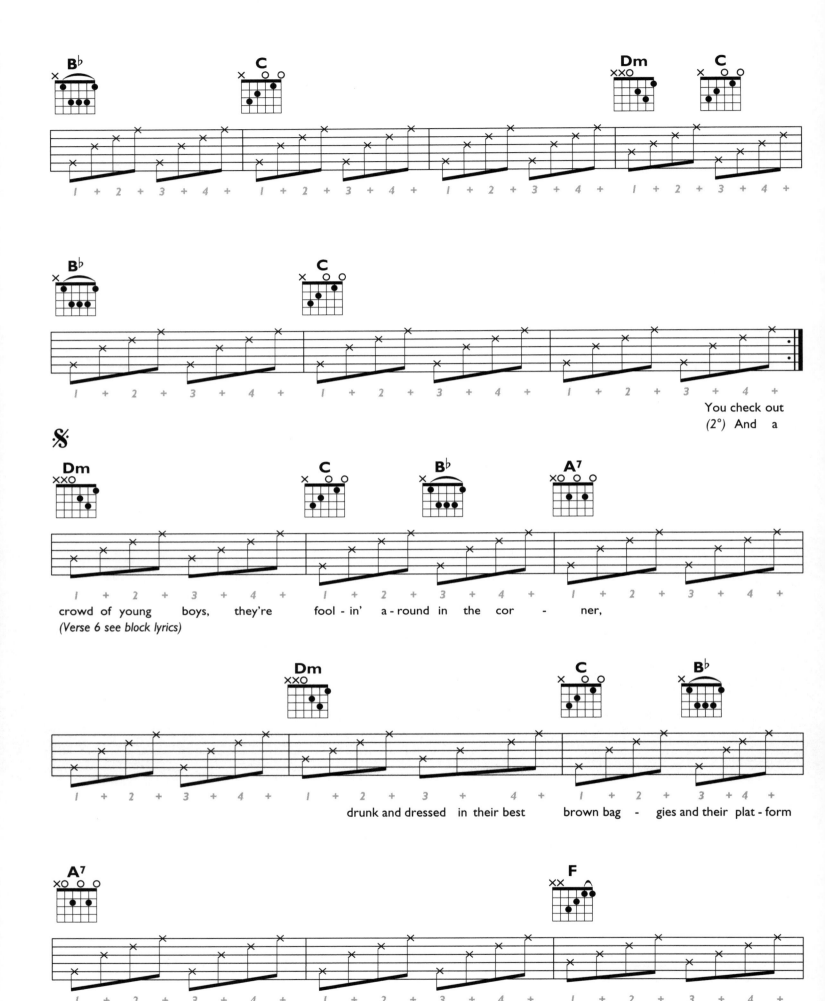

You check out
(2°) And a

crowd of young boys, they're fool-in' a-round in the cor - ner,
(Verse 6 see block lyrics)

drunk and dressed in their best brown bag - gies and their plat - form

soles. They don't give a damn

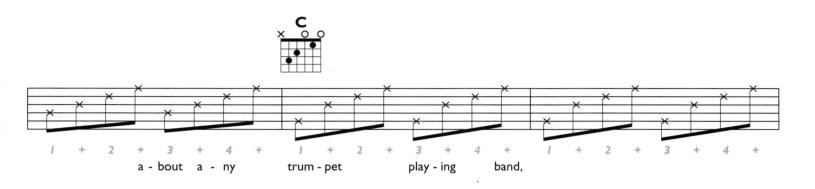

a - bout a - ny trum - pet play - ing band,

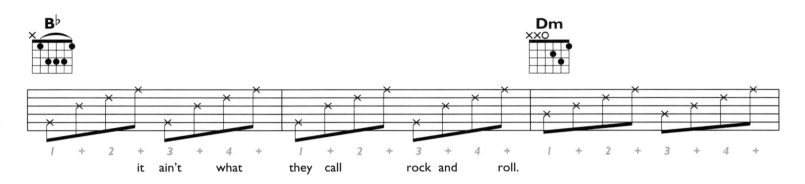

it ain't what they call rock and roll.

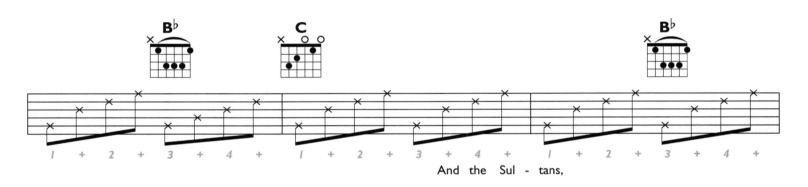

And the Sul - tans,

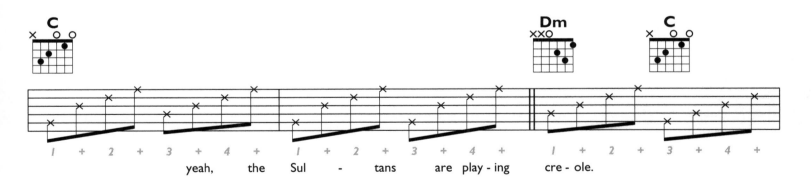

yeah, the Sul - tans are play - ing cre - ole.

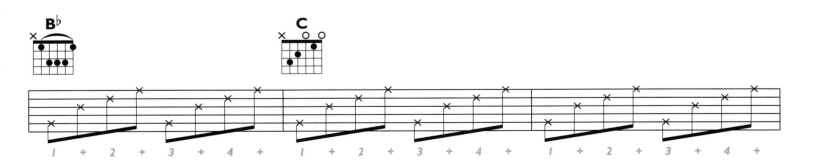

47

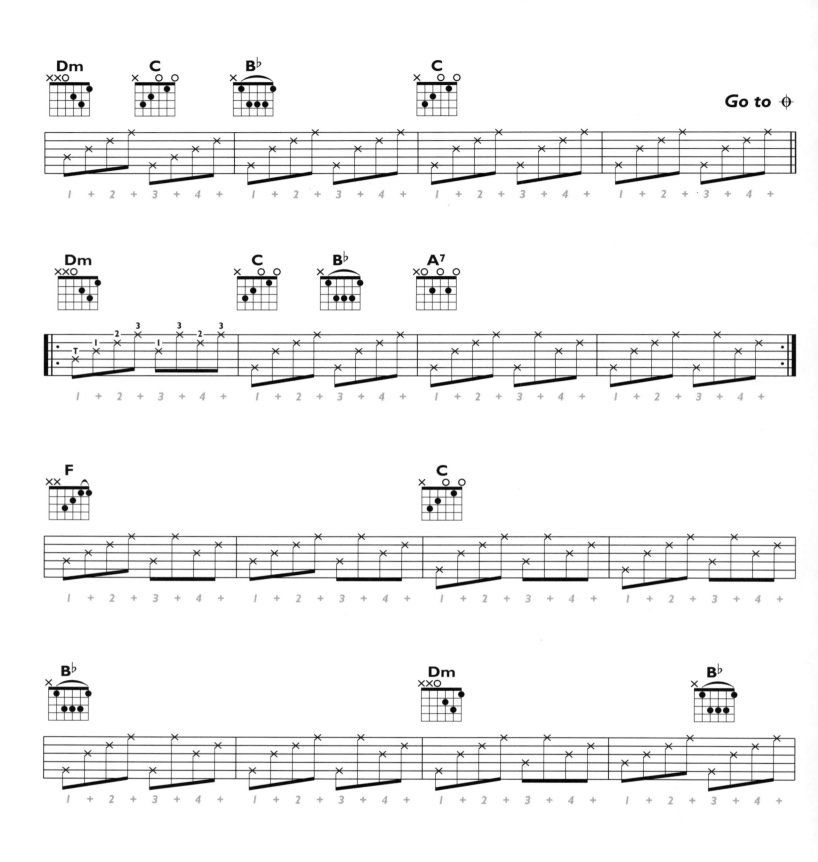

Go to ◊

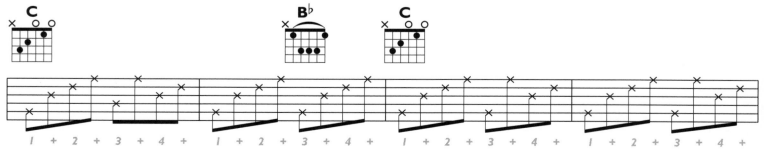

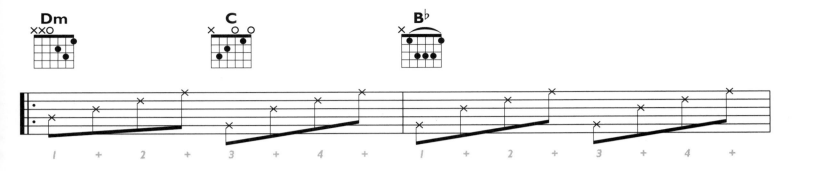

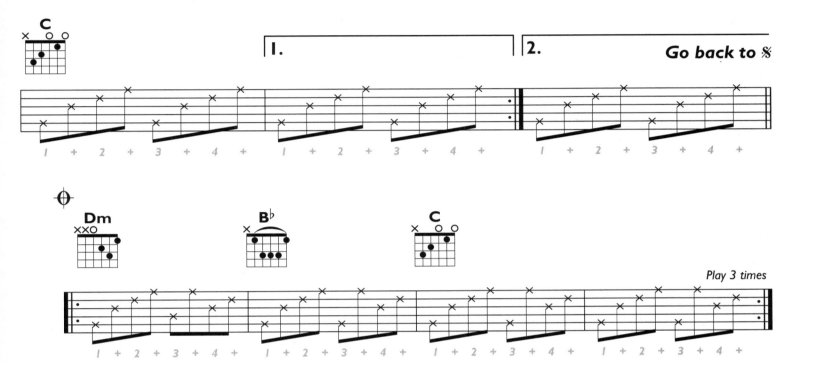

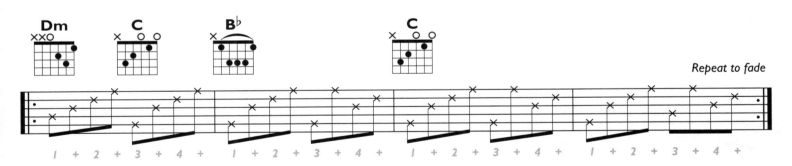

Verse 2:
You step inside, but you don't see too many faces
Coming in out of the rain to hear the jazz go down.
Too much competition too many other places.
But not too many horns can make that sound.
Way on down south, way on down south, London town.

Verse 3:
You check out Guitar George he knows all the chords.
Mind he's strictly rhythm he doesn't want to make it cry or sing.
And an old guitar is all he can afford,
When he gets up under the lights to play his thing.

Verse 4:
And Harry doesn't mind if he doesn't make the scene.
He's got a day-time job he's doing all right.
He can play honky-tonk like anything,
Saving it up for Friday night,
With the Sultans, with the Sultans Of Swing.

Verse 6:
And then the man he steps right up to the microphone.
And says at last just as the time bell rings.
"Thank you, goodnight now it's time to go home."
And he makes it fast with one more thing.
"We are the Sultans, we are the Sultans of Swing."

UNCHAINED MELODY

WORDS BY HY ZARET
MUSIC BY ALEX NORTH

This song needs a capo at the 5th fret. It has six counts per bar; look out for the variation in the picking in bar 4. At the end of the song there is a **Cm** chord (see photo below), which is the same shape as the **Bm** chord used earlier, moved up a fret.

When you get to the repeat bar (𝄇), go right back to the start of the song; then look for **Go to** ⊕ to take you to the outro of the song.

This Righteous Brothers' 1965 hit, produced by Phil Spector, was a hit again in the 1990s following its use in the film Ghost.

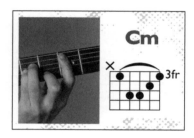

Cm

CAPO: 5th FRET

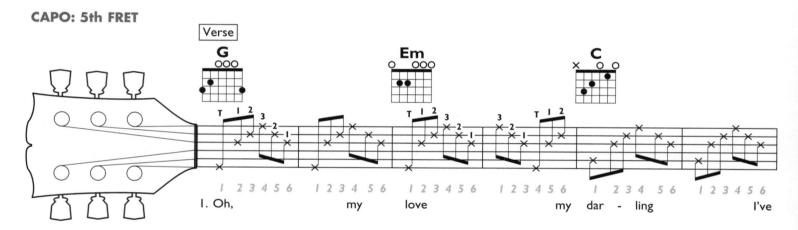

1. Oh,   my   love   my dar - ling   I've

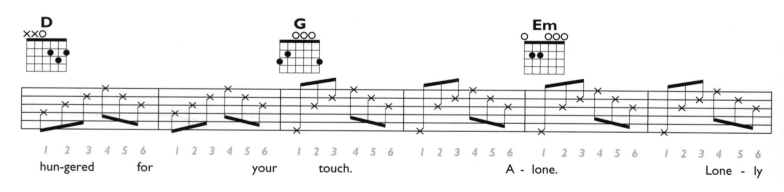

hun-gered   for   your   touch.   A - lone.   Lone - ly

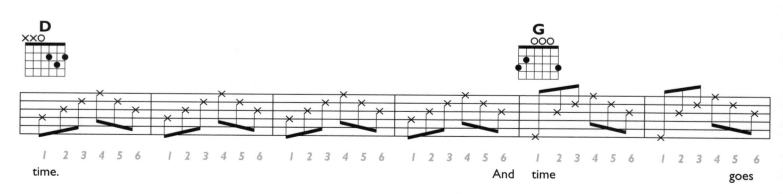

time.   And   time   goes

50

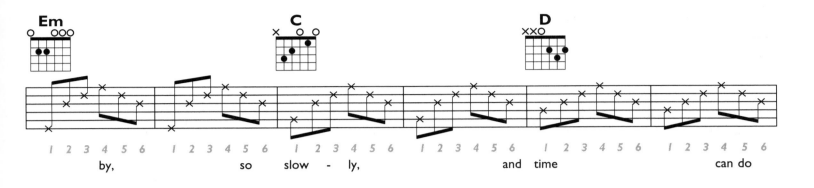

by, so slow - ly, and time can do

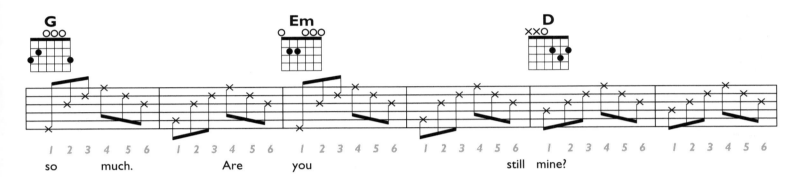

so much. Are you still mine?

Go to ⊕

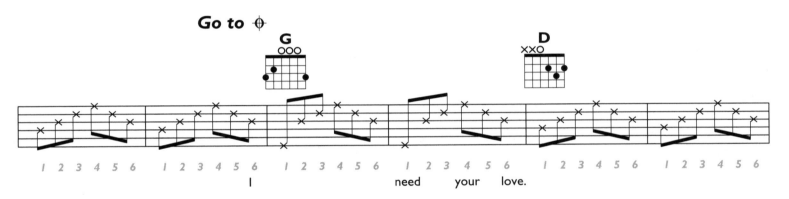

I need your love.

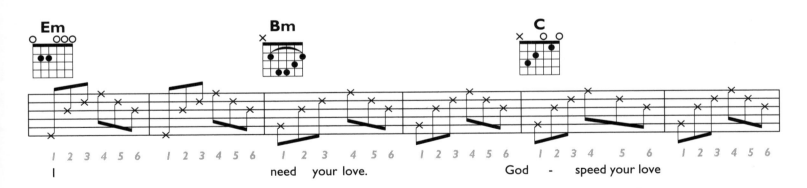

I need your love. God - speed your love

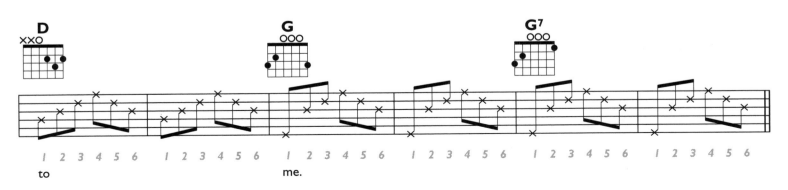

to me.

51

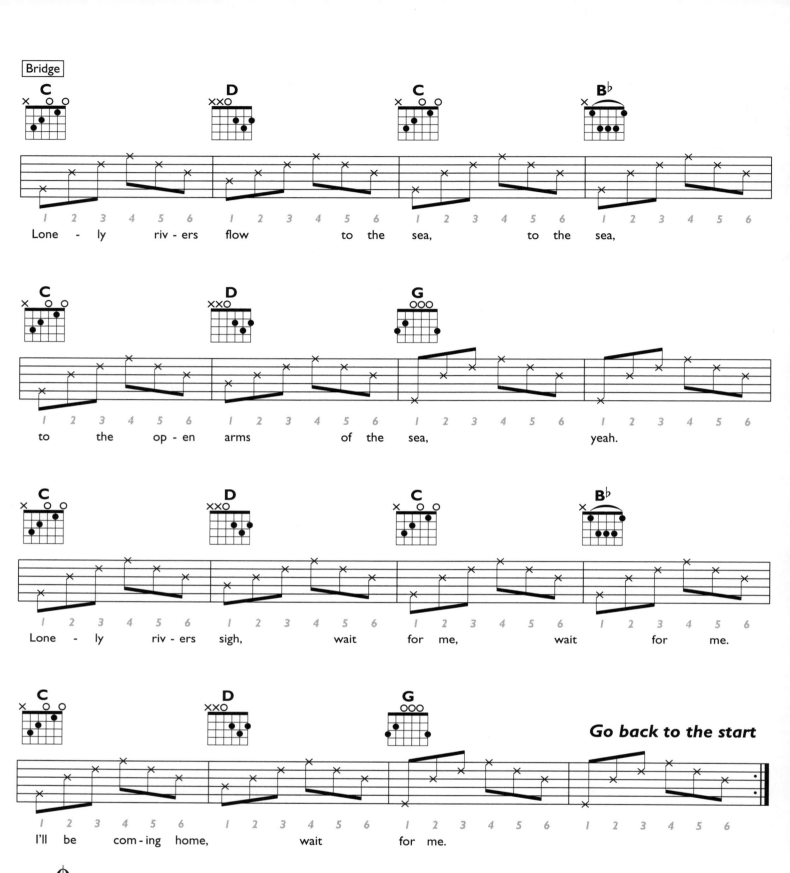

Bridge

C — **D** — **C** — **B♭**

Lone - ly riv - ers flow to the sea, to the sea,

C — **D** — **G**

to the op - en arms of the sea, yeah.

C — **D** — **C** — **B♭**

Lone - ly riv - ers sigh, wait for me, wait for me.

C — **D** — **G**

Go back to the start

I'll be com - ing home, wait for me.

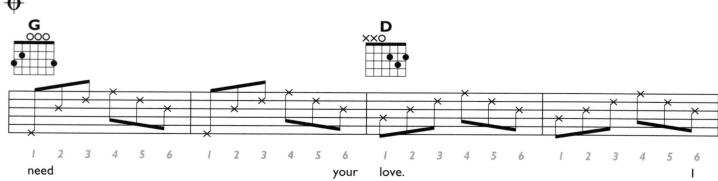

G — **D**

need your love.

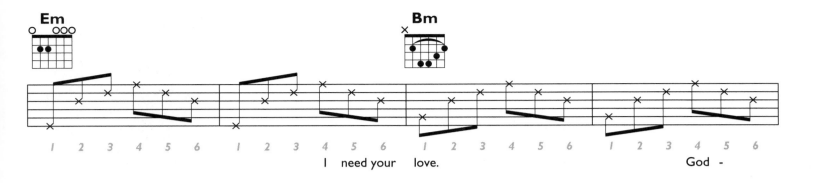

I   need your   love.   God -

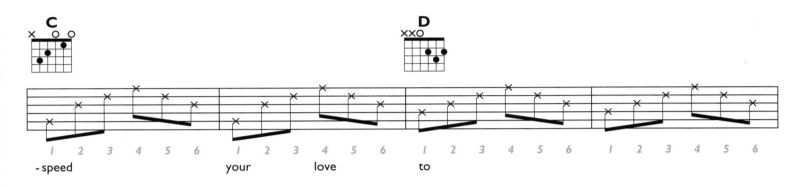

- speed   your   love   to

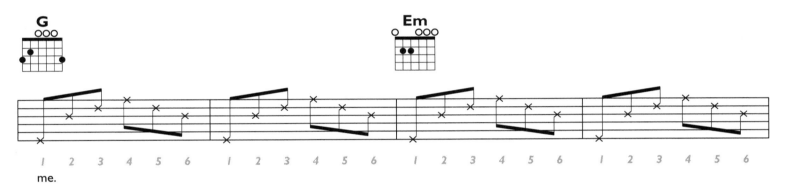

me.

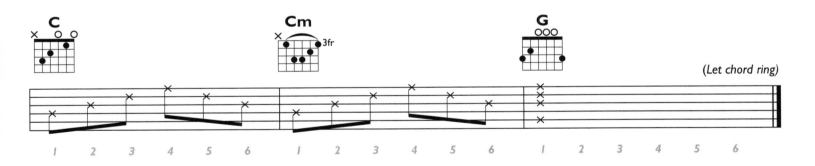

(Let chord ring)

YOU RAISE ME UP

WORDS AND MUSIC BY ROLF LOVLAND & BRENDAN GRAHAM

This inspirational song was a hit for Josh Groban in 2003.

Chords in this song such as **D/F#** and **A/C#** are used to create subtle variations in the harmony.

The picking pattern at the start of the song has two notes to be picked on every beat. **B/D** uses the same shape as **A/C#**, but up another fret. **A/E** is just like a normal **A** chord, but with the open 6th string as well. **B** is the same shape as **B♭**, moved up a fret.

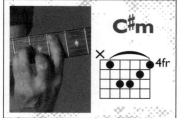

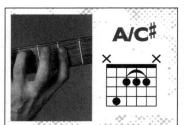
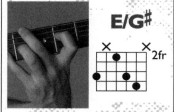

CAPO: 1st FRET

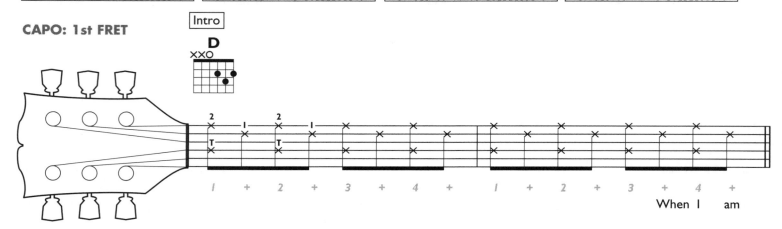

When I am

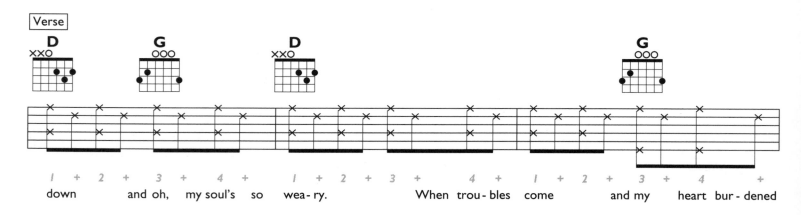

down   and oh, my soul's so wea-ry.   When trou-bles come   and my   heart bur-dened

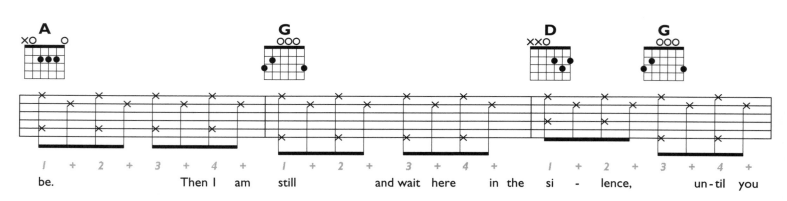

be.   Then I am   still   and wait here   in the si - lence,   un-til you

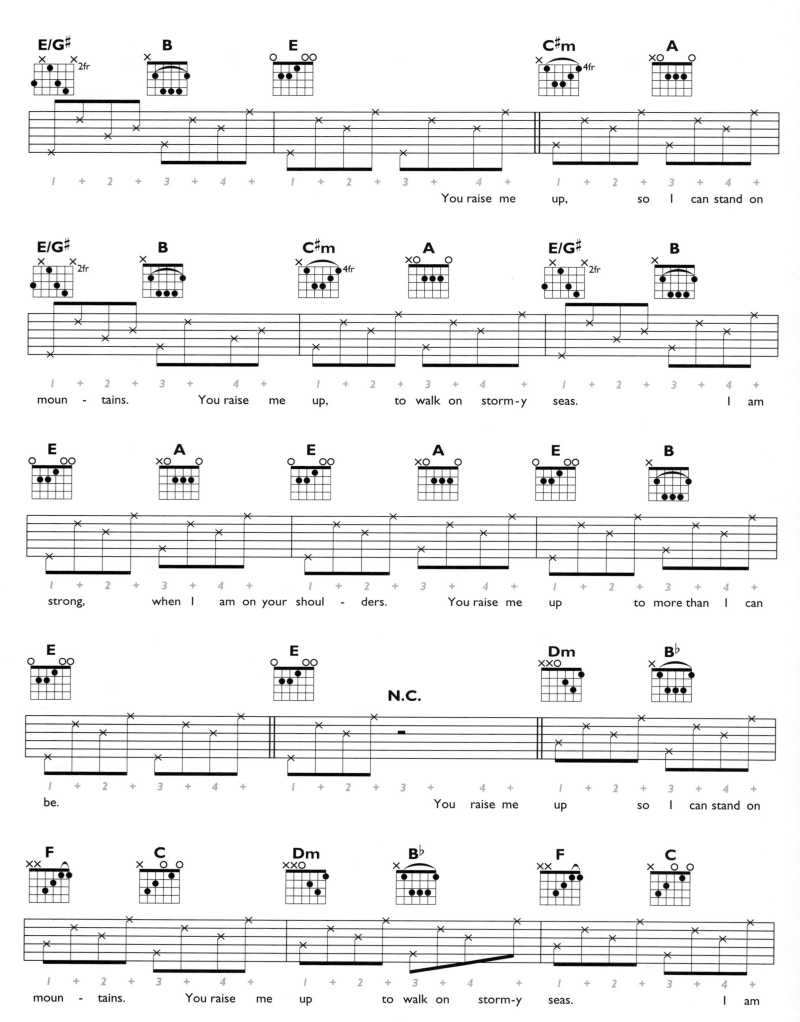

You raise me up, so I can stand on

moun - tains. You raise me up, to walk on storm-y seas. I am

strong, when I am on your shoul - ders. You raise me up to more than I can

be. You raise me up so I can stand on

moun - tains. You raise me up to walk on storm-y seas. I am

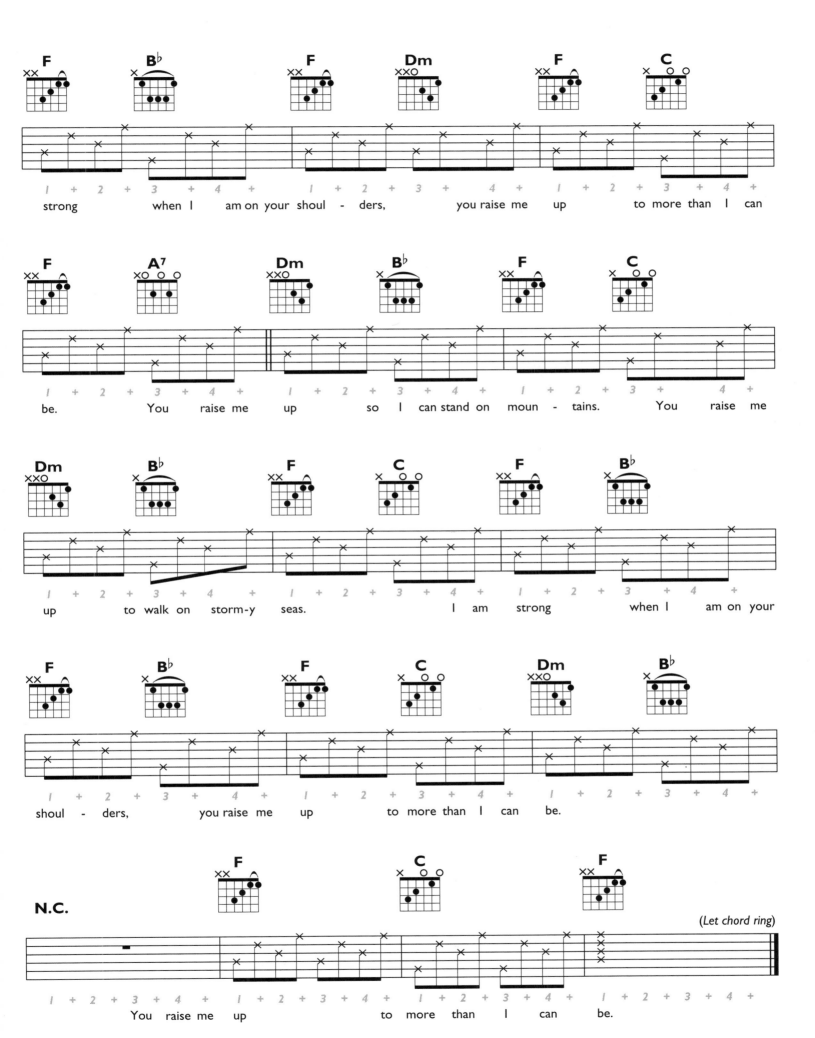

YOU GIVE ME SOMETHING

WORDS AND MUSIC BY FRANCIS WHITE & JAMES MORRISON

A♭ and **Fm** are barre chords. To finger **C/G**, start with an **Am** shape, and then move your 3rd finger over to the 6th string; see the photo below.

This 2006 song was James Morrison's debut single.

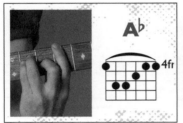

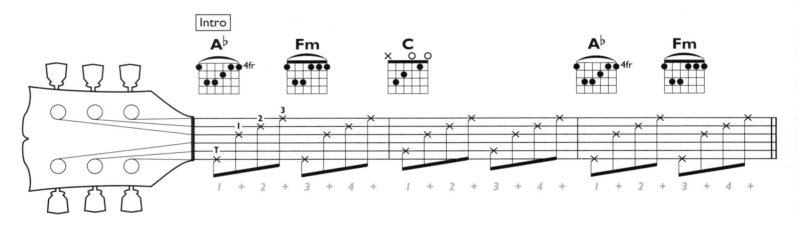

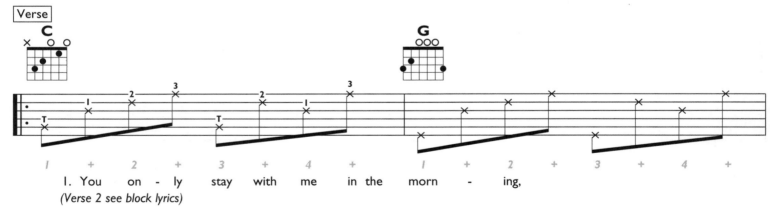

1. You on - ly stay with me in the morn - ing,

(Verse 2 see block lyrics)

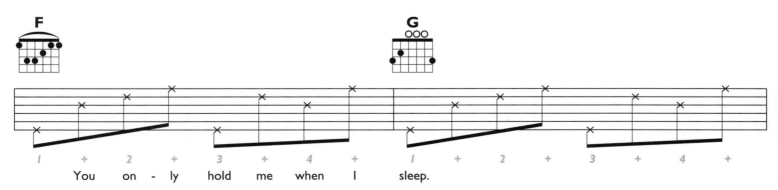

You on - ly hold me when I sleep.

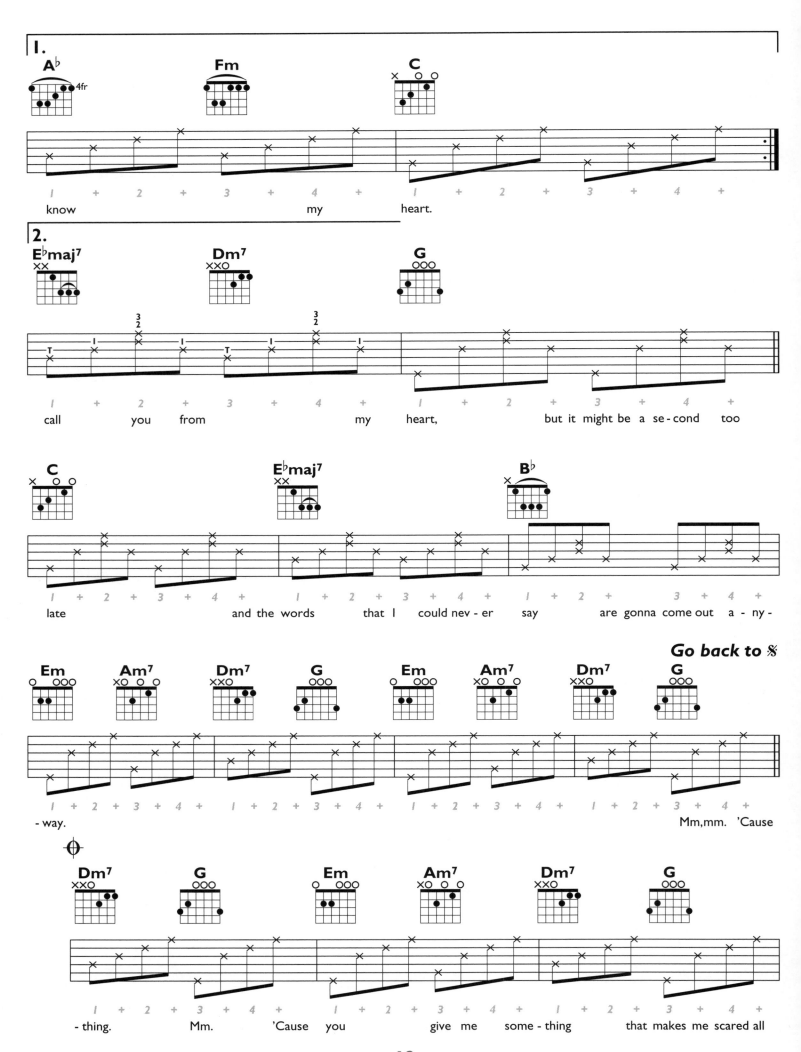

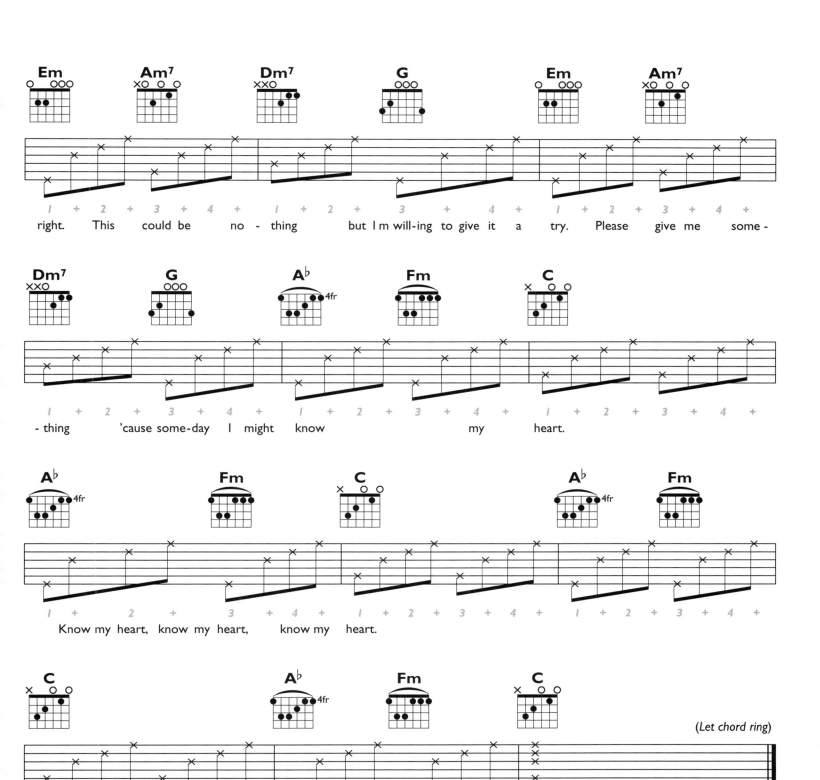

right. This could be no - thing but I m will-ing to give it a try. Please give me some -

- thing 'cause some-day I might know my heart.

Know my heart, know my heart, know my heart.

(Let chord ring)

Verse 2:
You already waited up for hours,
Just to spend a little time alone with me.
And I can say I've never bought you flowers,
I can't work out what they mean.
I never thought that I'd love someone,
That was someone else's dream.

HERE, THERE AND EVERYWHERE

WORDS AND MUSIC BY JOHN LENNON & PAUL McCARTNEY

This short song has a lot of chords! As ever, practise shifting between each shape slowly at first.

This Beatles' classic first appeared on the 1966 album Revolver. It is reputed to have been inspired by God Only Knows by the Beach Boys.

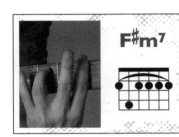 F#m7 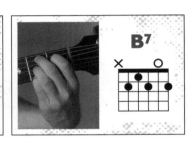 B7 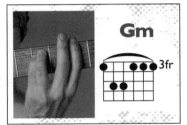 Gm

Intro

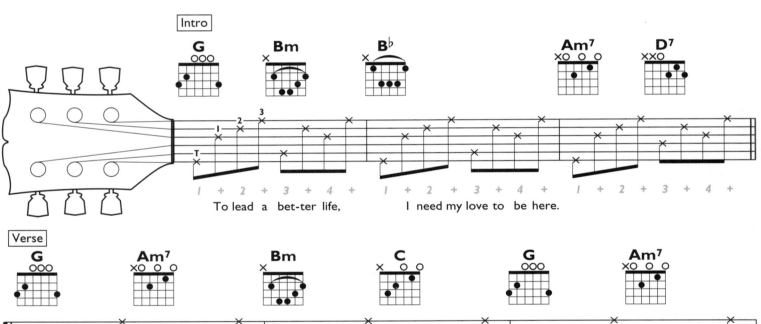

To lead a bet-ter life,   I need my love to be here.

Verse

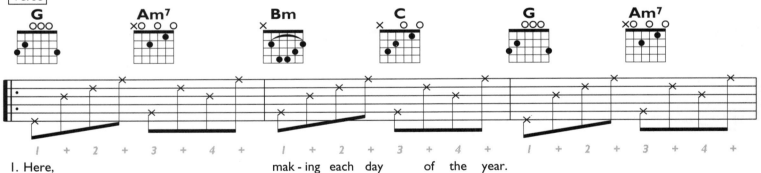

1. Here,   mak - ing each day   of   the   year.
(Verse 2 see block lyric)

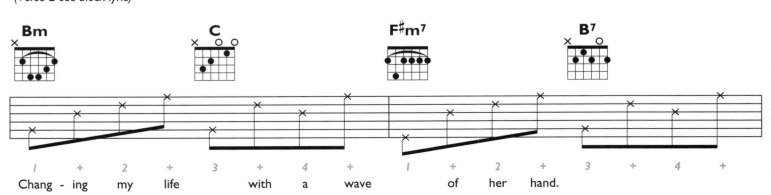

Chang - ing   my   life   with   a   wave   of   her   hand.

62

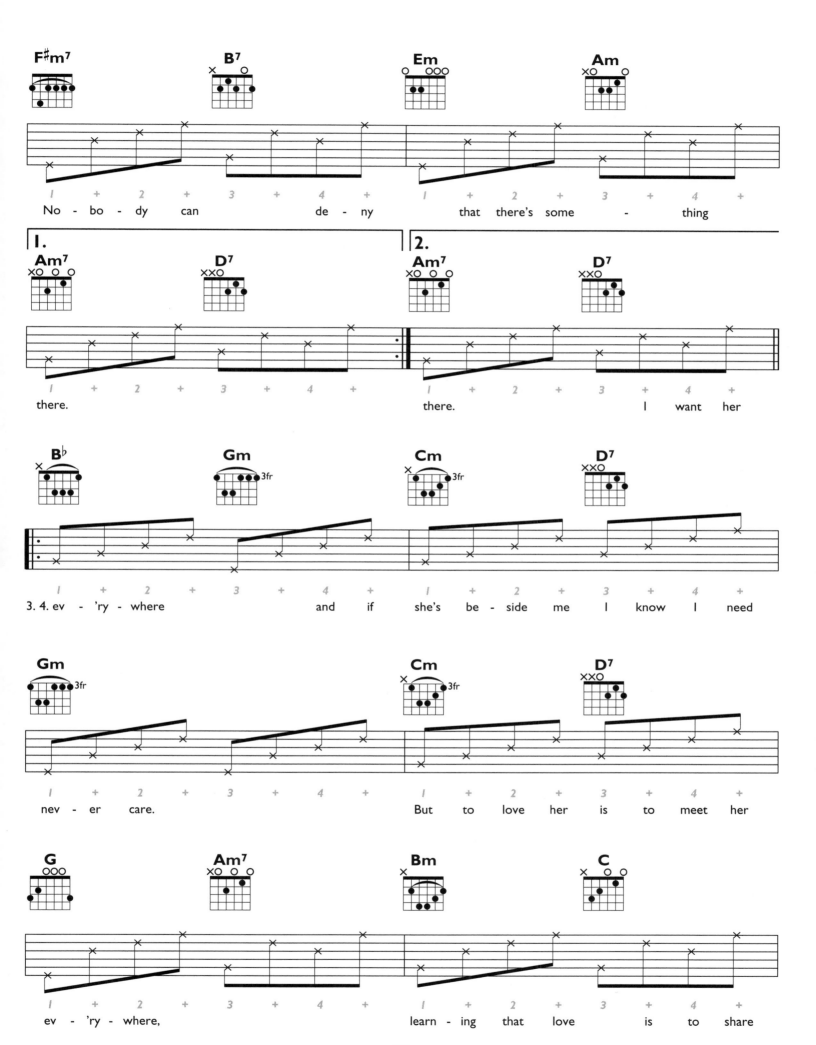

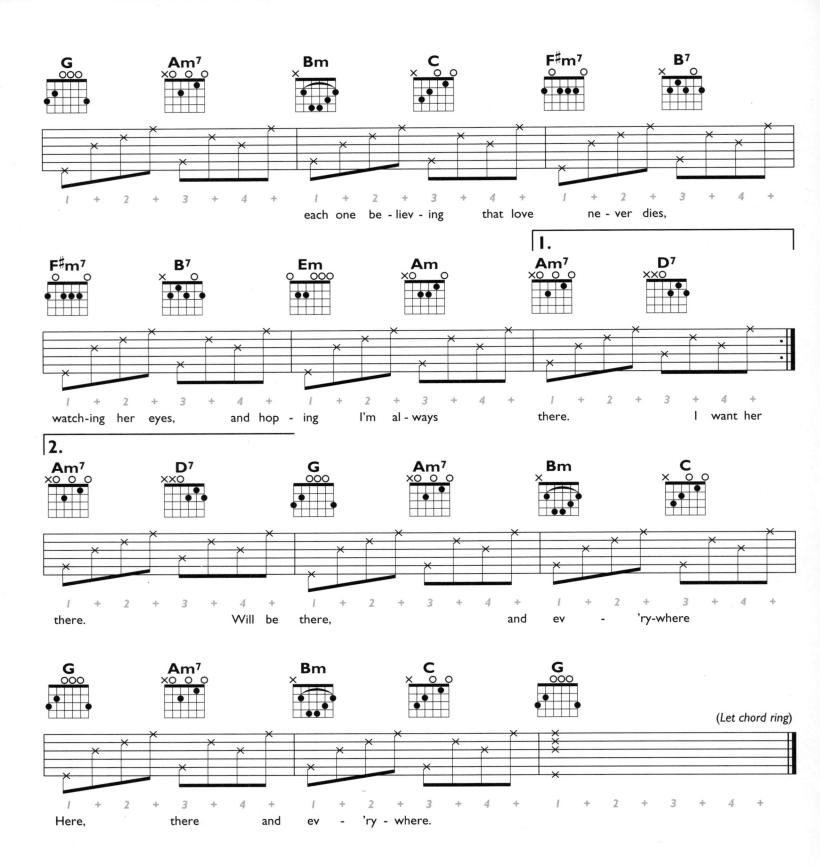

Verse 2:
There, running my hands through her hair.
Both of us thinking how good it can be,
Someone is speaking,
But she doesn't know he's there.

2 3 4 5 6 7 8 9
2/09 (169021)